HAL•LEONARD

LISTEN ONLINE

PREVIEW AUDIO CLIPS

PIANO • VOCAL • GUITAR

The Wedding Reception SONGBOOK

ISBN 978-1-4584-4073-0

HAL•LEONARD® CORPORATION

7777 W. BLUEMOUND RD. P.O. BOX 13819 MILWAUKEE, WI 53213

Visit Hal Leonard Online at
www.halleonard.com

Contents by Category

SONGS FOR DINNER & LIGHT DANCING

COUPLE'S FIRST DANCE

FATHER/DAUGHTER DANCE

Alphabetical Listing

EVERYTHING

Words and Music by AMY FOSTER-GILLIES,
MICHAEL BUBLÉ and ALAN CHANG

Moderately fast

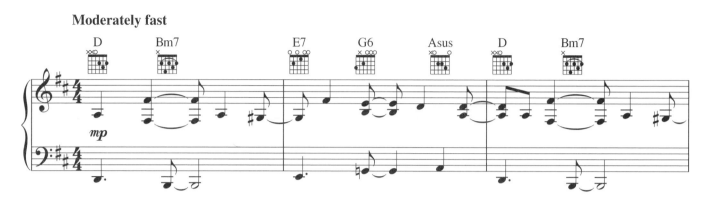

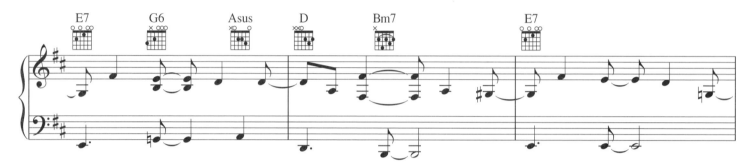

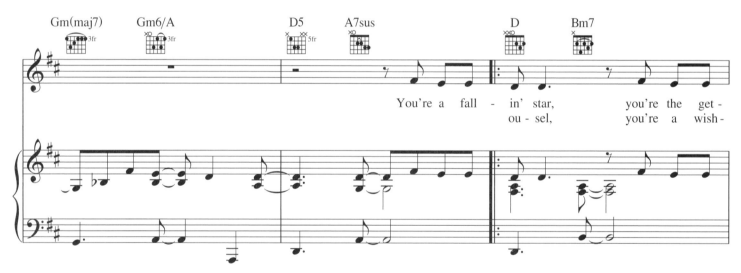

You're a fall- in' star, _____ you're the get-
ou- sel, _____ you're a wish-

a - way car, _____ you're the line _____ in the sand _____ when I go
ing well, _____ and you light _____ me _____ up _____ when you ring

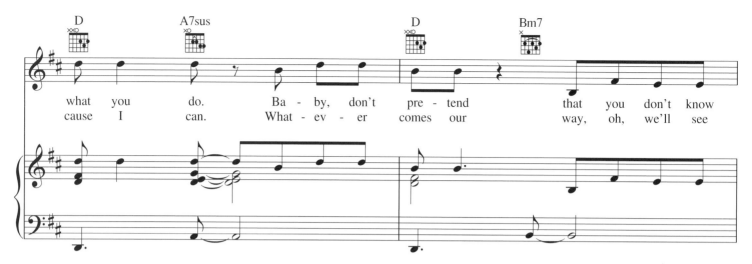

what you do. Baby, don't pre-tend that you don't know
cause I can. What-ev-er comes our way, oh, we'll see

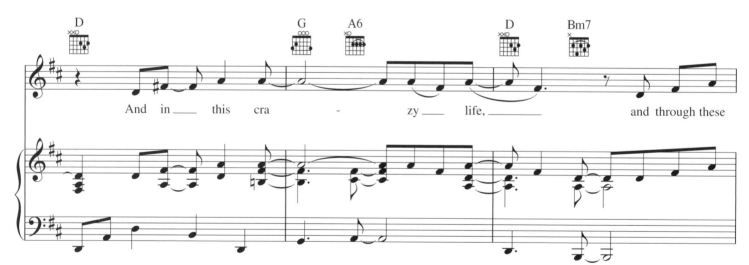

it's true, 'cause you can see it when I look at you.
it through. And you know _____ that's what our love can do.

And in ____ this cra - zy ____ life, _____ and through these

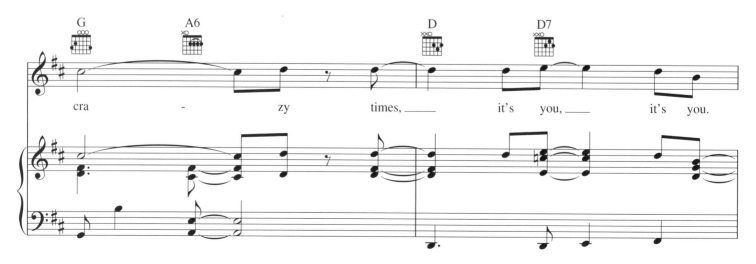

cra - zy times, ____ it's you, ____ it's you.

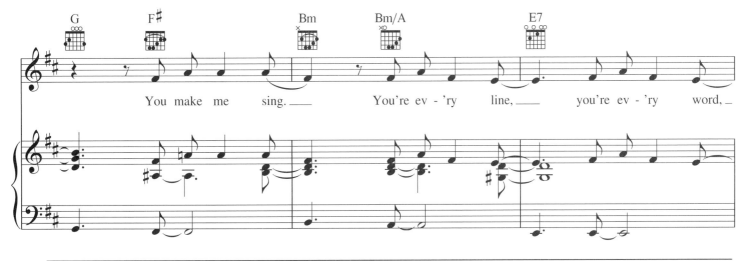

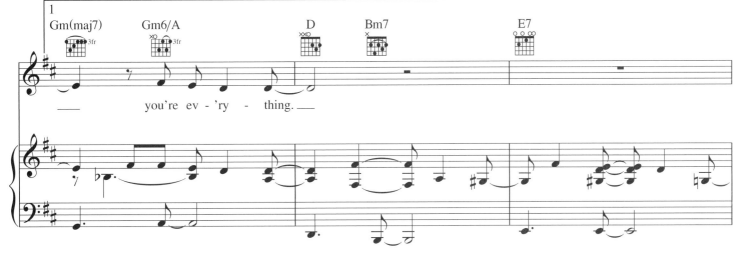

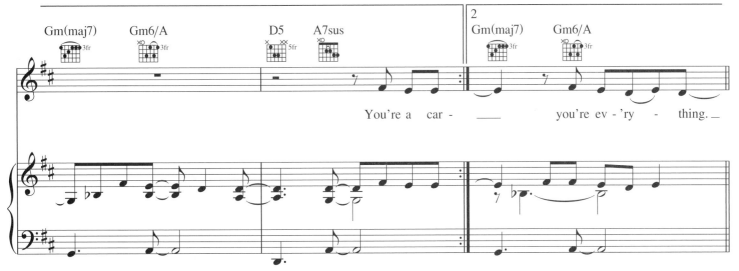

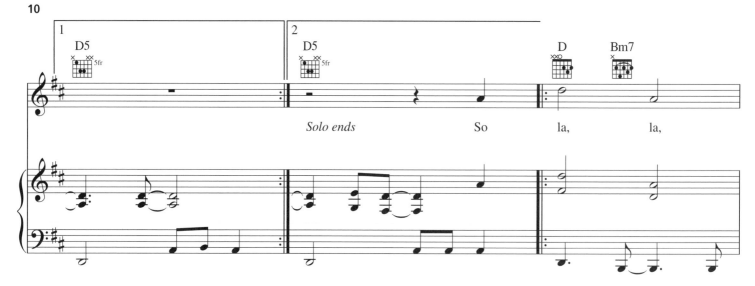

Solo ends   So   la,   la,

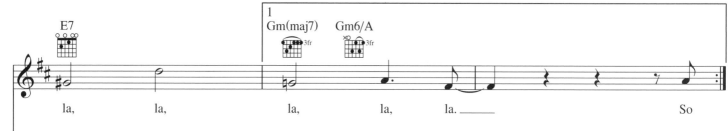

la,   la,   la,   la,   la. _____   So

la,   la,   la.   And in ___ this   cra - zy   life, __

___   and   through   these   cra - zy   times, __

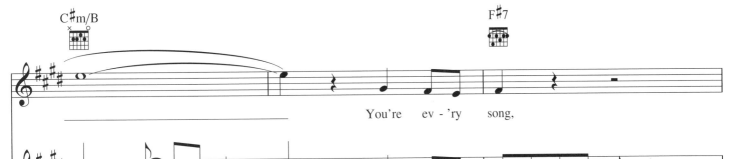

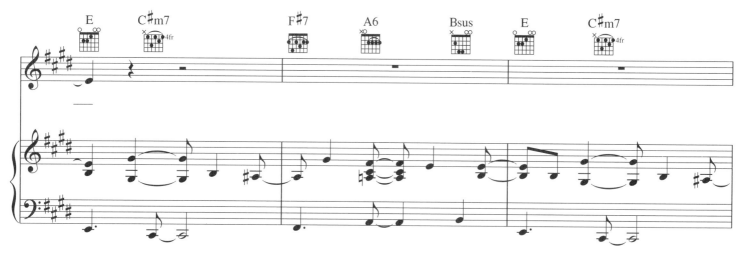

So la, la, la, la,

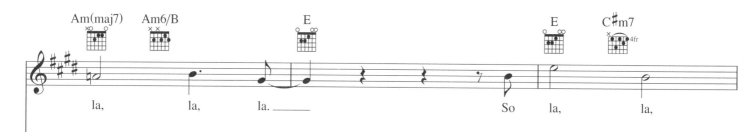

la, la, la. _____ So la, la,

la, la, la, la, la, la, la, la, la. _____

FIELDS OF GOLD

Music and Lyrics by
STING

You'll re-mem-ber me, when the west wind moves _ up a-
stay with me, when will you be my love _ a-

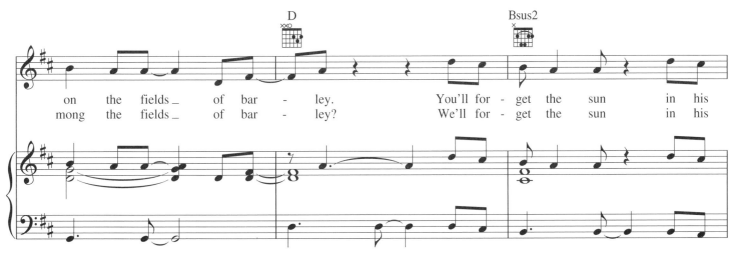

on the fields _ of bar - ley. You'll for - get the sun in his
mong the fields _ of bar - ley? We'll for - get the sun in his

jeal - ous sky as we walk in fields __ of gold.
jeal - ous sky as we lie in fields __ of gold.

So she
See the

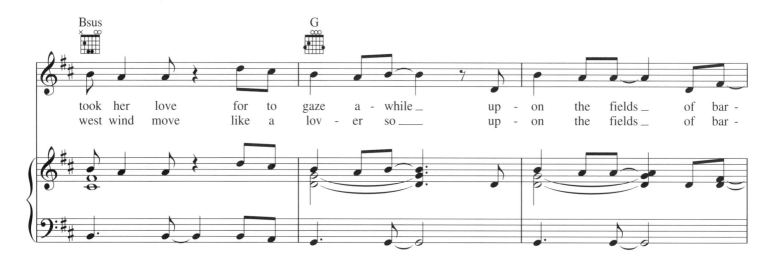

took her love for to gaze a - while __ up - on the fields __ of bar -
west wind move like a lov - er so ___ up - on the fields __ of bar -

- ley. In his arms she fell as her hair came down a - mong __
- ley. Feel her bod - y rise when you kiss her mouth a - mong __

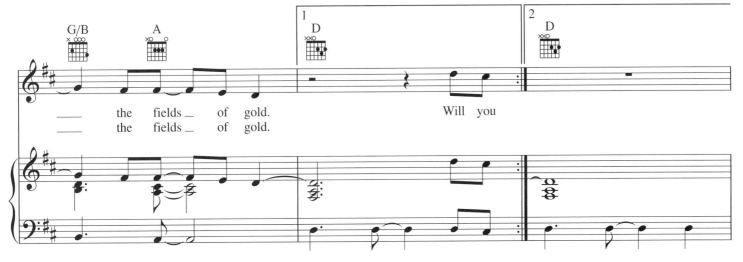

the fields of gold.
the fields of gold. Will you

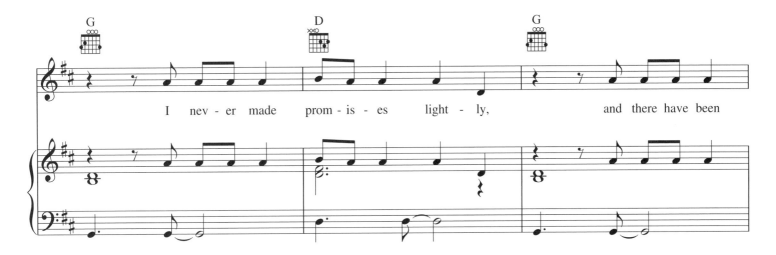

I never made promises lightly, and there have been

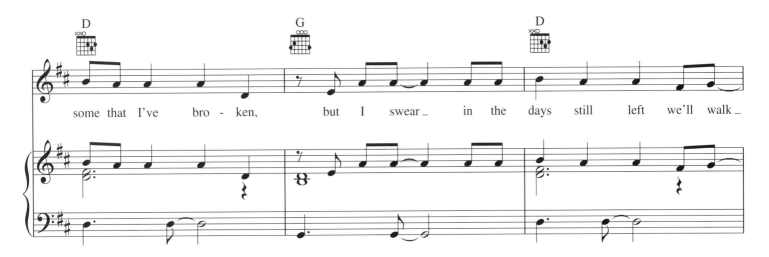

some that I've broken, but I swear in the days still left we'll walk

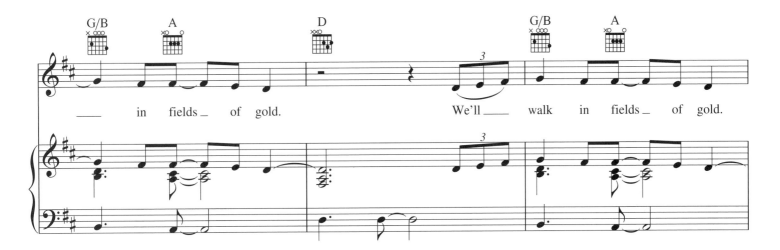

in fields of gold. We'll walk in fields of gold.

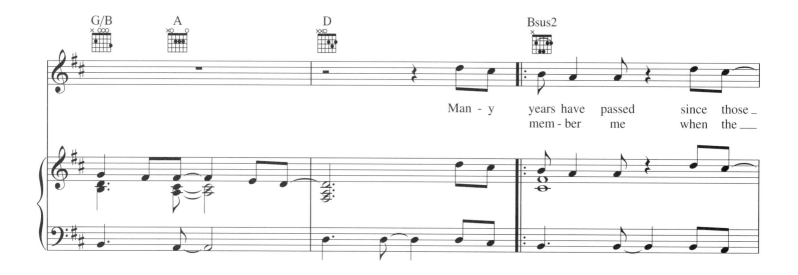

Man - y years have passed since those _ summer days
mem - ber me when the ___ west wind moves

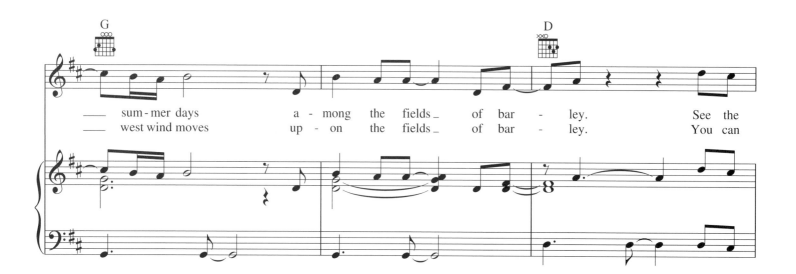

___ sum - mer days a - mong the fields _ of bar - ley. See the
___ west wind moves up - on the fields _ of bar - ley. You can

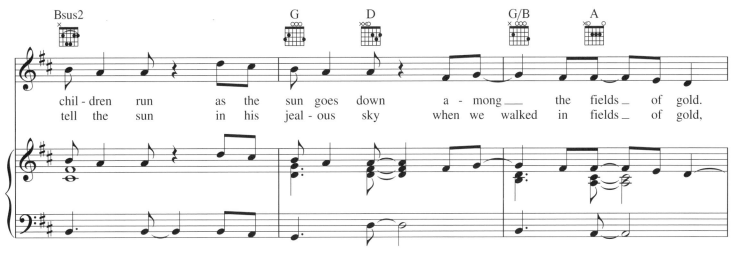

chil - dren run as the sun goes down a - mong __ the fields __ of gold.
tell the sun in his jeal - ous sky when we walked in fields __ of gold,

You'll re -

when __ we walked in fields __ of gold,

when we walked in fields __ of gold.

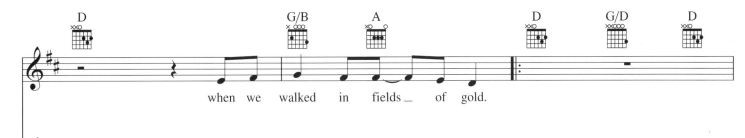

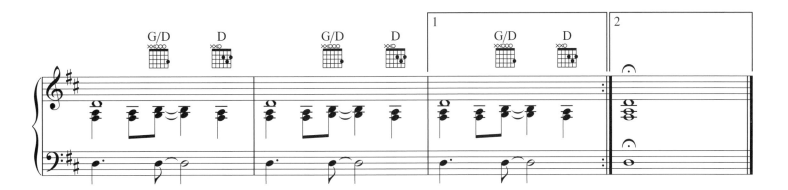

JUST THE WAY YOU ARE

Words and Music by
BILLY JOEL

Moderately, in 2

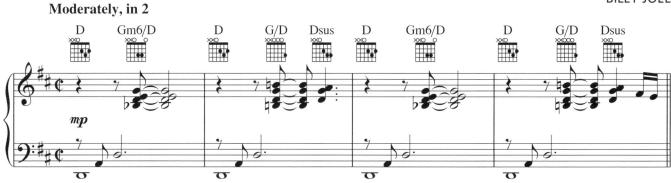

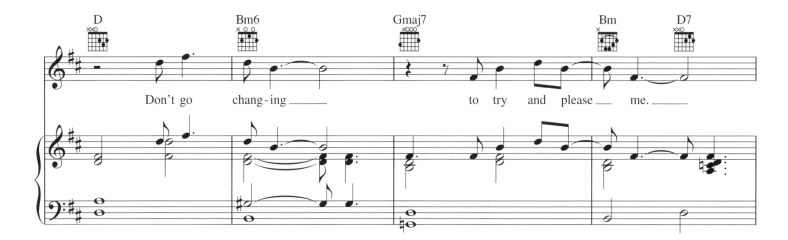

Don't go chang-ing ____ to try and please ____ me. ____

You nev-er let me down ____ be-fore. ____ Mm, ____ mm.

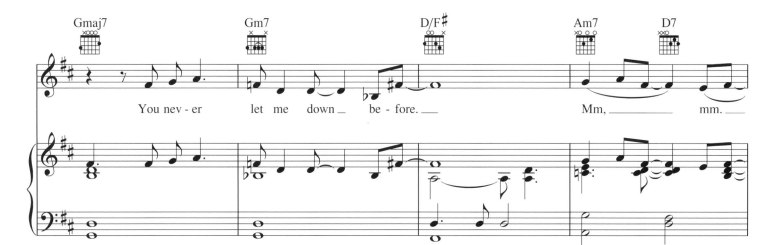

____ Don't i-mag - ine ____ you're too fa - mil - iar,

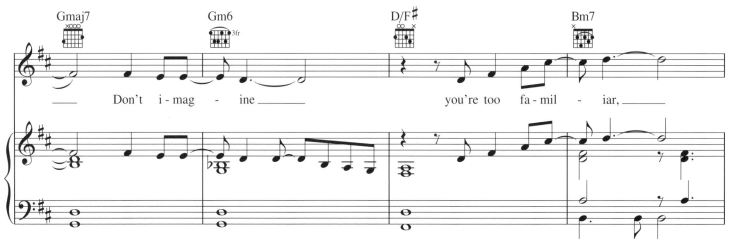

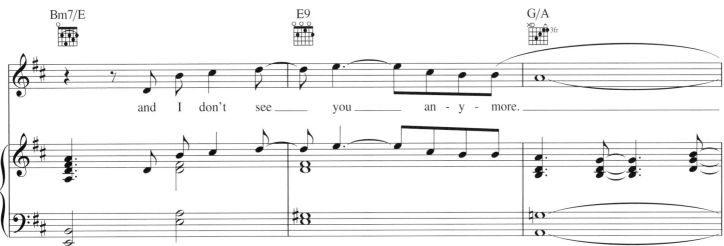

and I don't see ___ you ___ an - y - more. ___

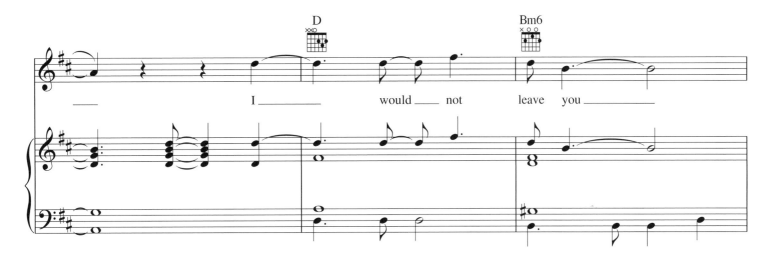

___ I ___ would ___ not leave you ___

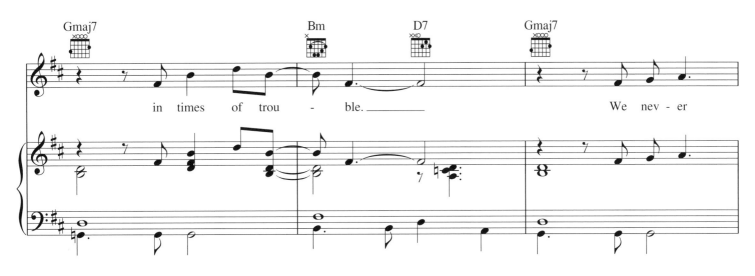

in times of trou - ble. ___ We nev - er

could have come ___ this ___ far. ___ Mm, mm. ___

I took the good ___ times; ___ I'll take the bad ___ times. ___

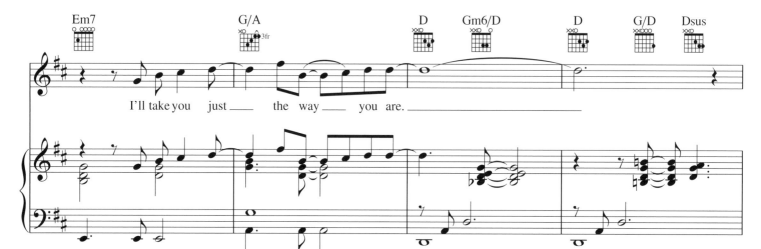

I'll take you just ___ the way ___ you are. _____

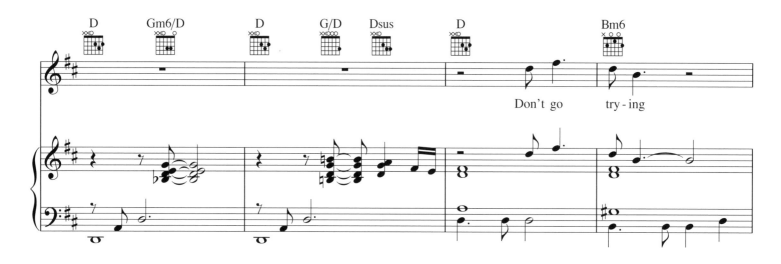

Don't go try - ing

some ___ new fash - ion. ___ Don't change the col - or of ___ your ___ hair. ___

Mm, _____ mm. _____ You al - ways have my

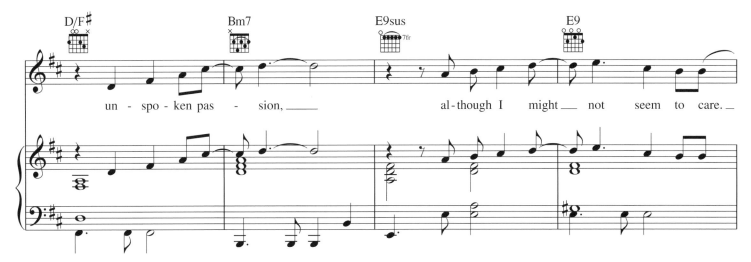

un - spo - ken pas - sion, _____ al - though I might __ not seem to care. __

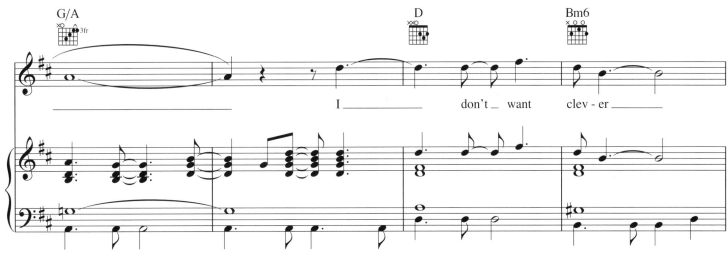

I _____ don't __ want clev - er _____

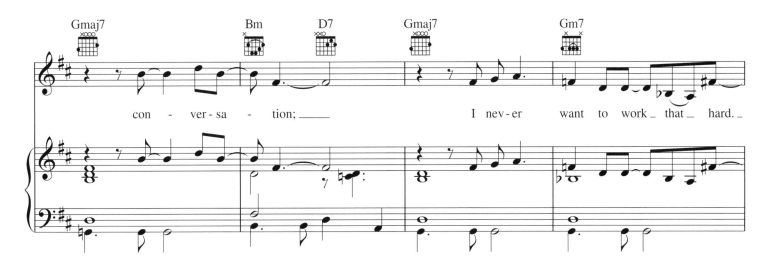

con - ver - sa - tion; _____ I nev - er want to work __ that __ hard. __

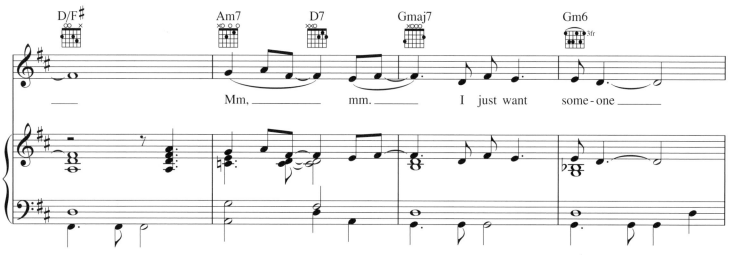

Mm, _____ mm. _____ I just want some-one _____

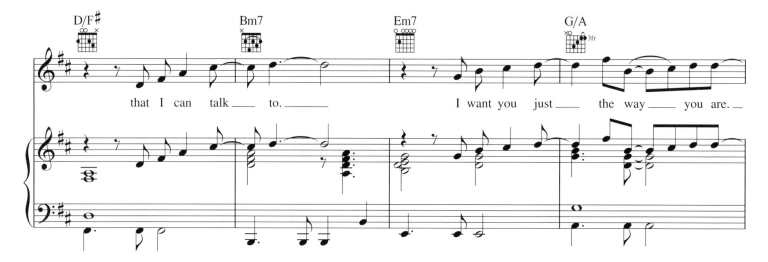

that I can talk ____ to. _____ I want you just ____ the way ____ you are. _____

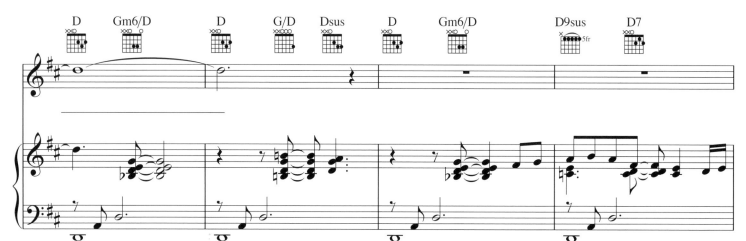

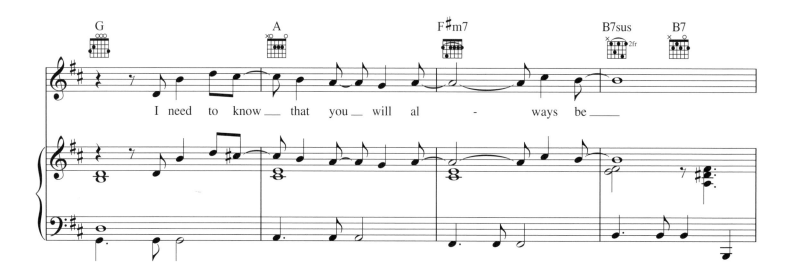

I need to know ____ that you ____ will al - ways be _____

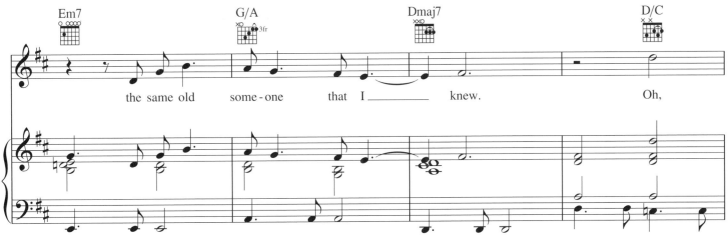

the same old some-one that I _____ knew. Oh,

what will it take ___ till you __ be - lieve _____ in me ___

the way that I _____ be - lieve __ in you? _____ I _____

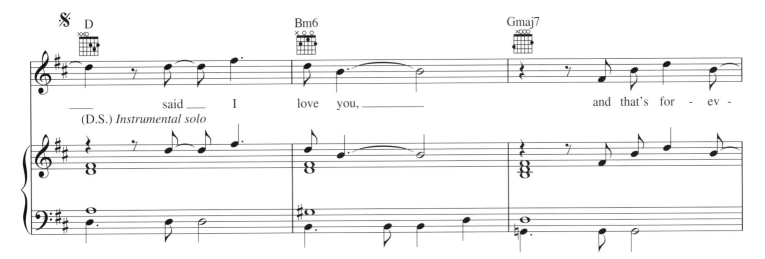

___ said ___ I love you, _____ and that's for - ev -

(D.S.) *Instrumental solo*

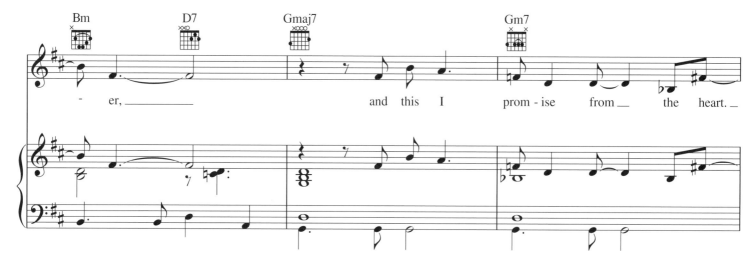

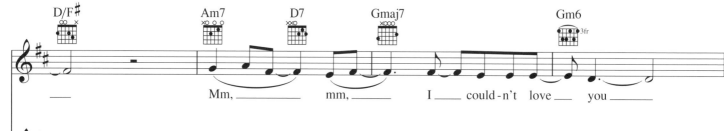

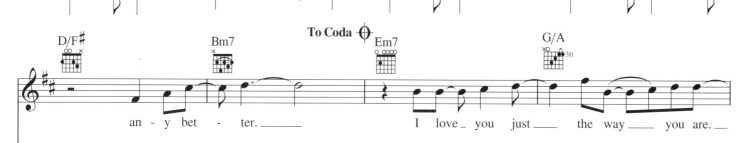

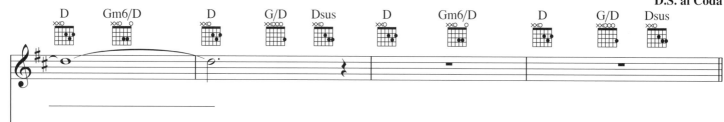

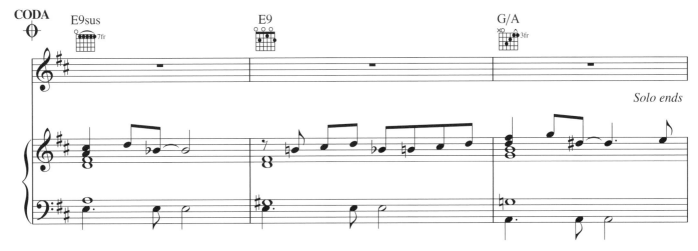

Solo ends

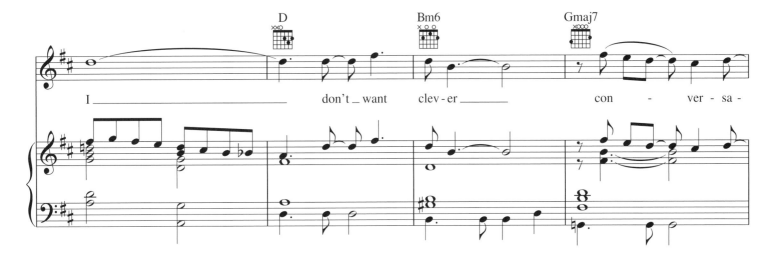

I don't _ want clev-er _____ con - ver-sa-

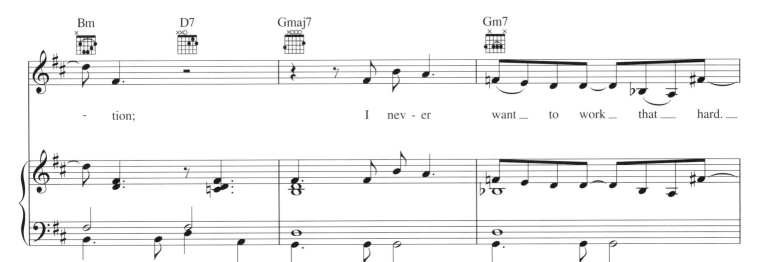

-tion; I nev-er want _ to work _ that _ hard. _

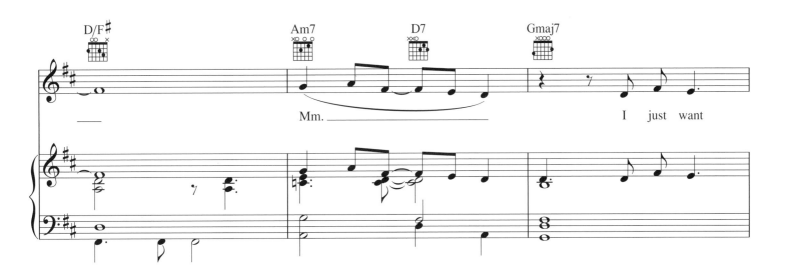

Mm. _____ I just want

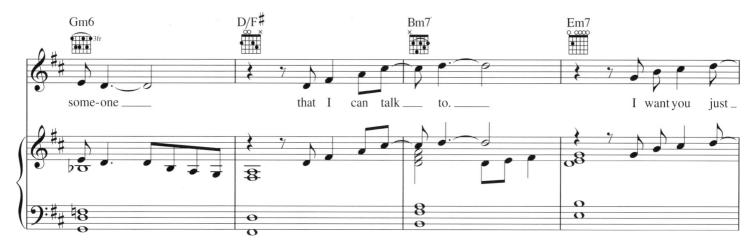

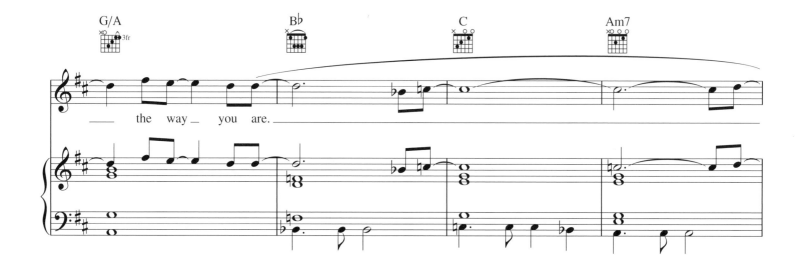

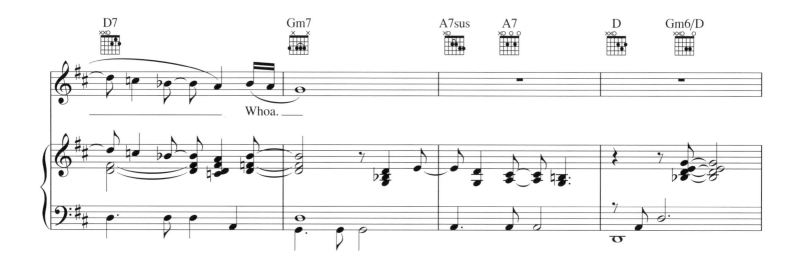

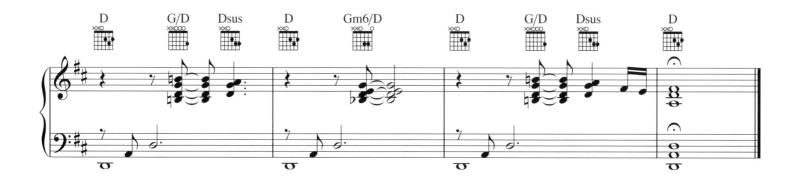

THE WAY YOU LOOK TONIGHT

from SWING TIME

Words by DOROTHY FIELDS
Music by JEROME KERN

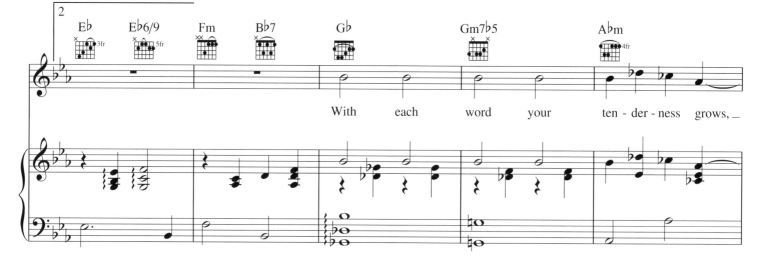

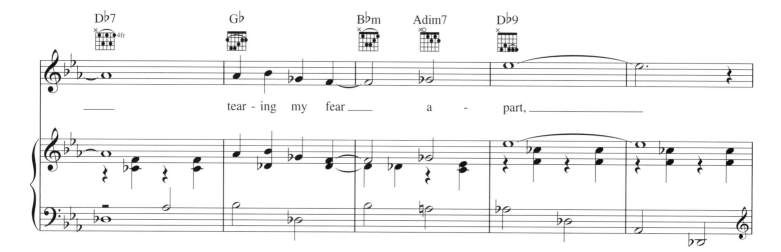

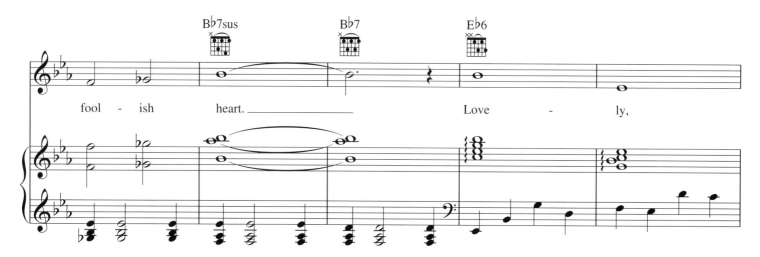

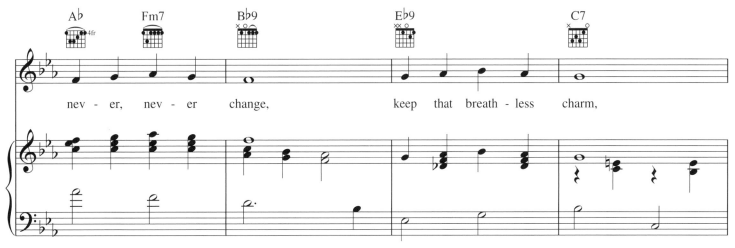

nev - er, nev - er change, keep that breath - less charm,

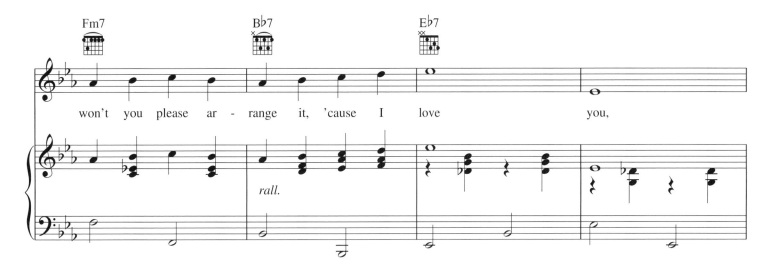

won't you please ar - range it, 'cause I love you,

rall.

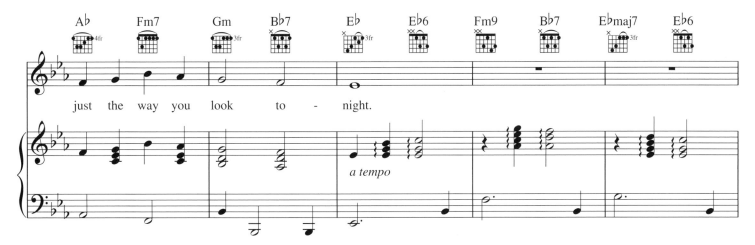

just the way you look to - night.

a tempo

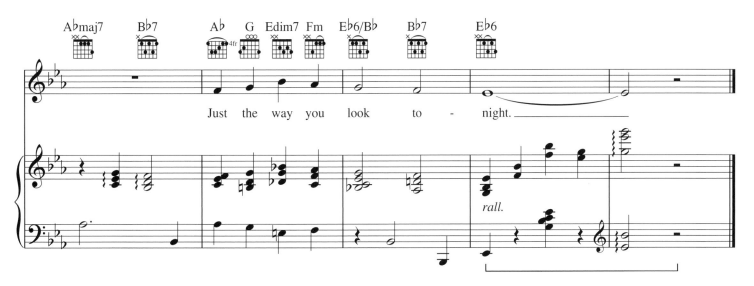

Just the way you look to - night._____

rall.

LUCKY

Words and Music by JASON MRAZ,
COLBIE CAILLAT and TIMOTHY FAGAN

Female vocal sung one octave lower than written.

*Substitute half rest on D.S.

world keeps __ spin - ning 'round, you hold _____ me right _ here, right now.

CODA

Oo, _____

oo. _____ Oo, _____

oo. _____ Oo. _____

(I've Had)
THE TIME OF MY LIFE
from DIRTY DANCING

Words and Music by FRANKE PREVITE,
JOHN DeNICOLA and DONALD MARKOWITZ

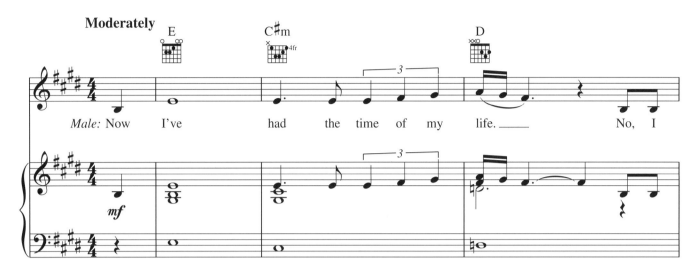

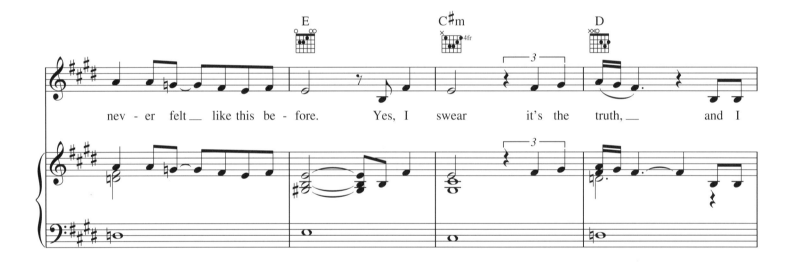

sy. _____ *Both:* Now with

pas - sion in our eyes _____ there's no way we could_ dis - guise _____ it se - cret -

ly. _____ So we

take each oth - er's hand _____ 'cause we seem to un - der - stand_ the ur - gen -

cy.

Male: Just __ re - mem - ber, *Female:* you're the

one thing *Male:* I can't get e - nough __ of. *Female:* So I'll tell you

some - thing: *Both:* this could be love. Be - cause I've __ had __

__ the time of my life. ____ No, I nev - er felt __ this way be -

fore. Yes, I swear it's the truth, _____ and I owe it all to you. _____

Male: Hey, ba - by.

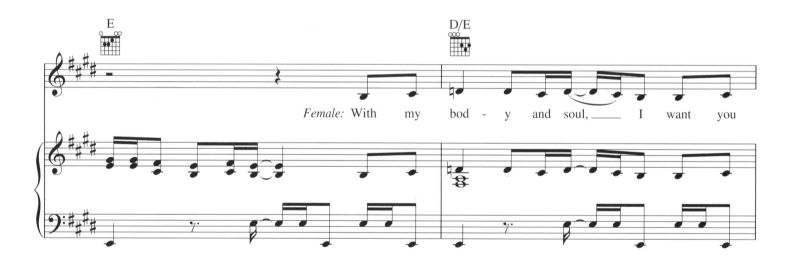

Female: With my bod - y and soul, _____ I want you

more than you'll ev - er know. _ *Male:* So we'll

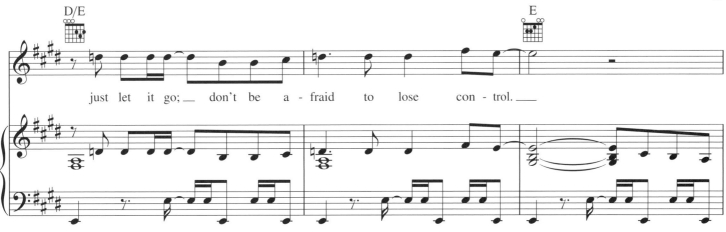

just let it go; __ don't be a-fraid to lose con-trol. __

Female: Yes, I know what's on __ your mind when you say stay with me to-

night. ____ *Male:* Stay _ with me. Just re-mem-ber, you're the

one thing _ *Female:* I _____ can't get e-nough of. *Male:* So I'll tell you

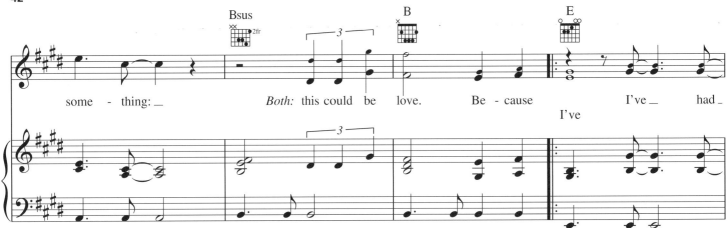

some - thing: __ *Both:* this could be love. Be - cause I've __ had __
I've

__ the time of my life. __ No, I nev - er felt __ this way be -
had the time of my life. __ And I've searched through ev - 'ry o - pen

fore. Yes, I swear it's the truth, _____ and I
door till I've found the __ truth, _____ and I

owe it all to you. __ 'Cause __ owe it all to you. _____

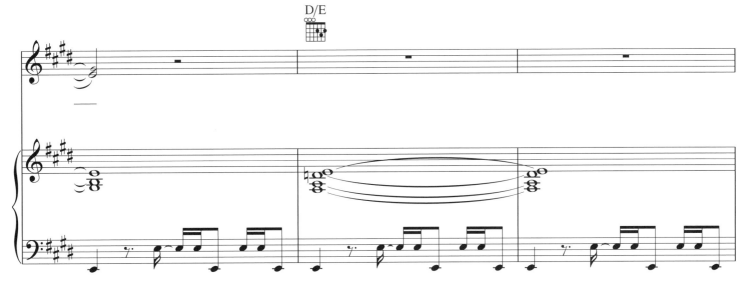

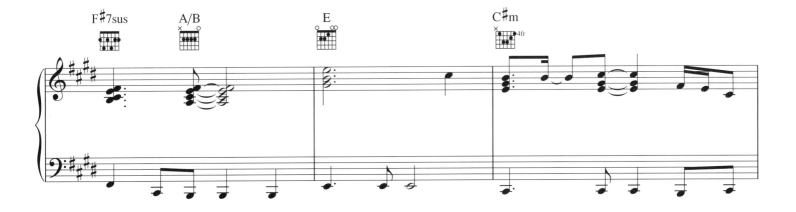

44

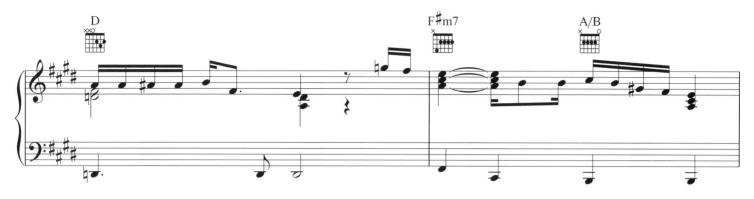

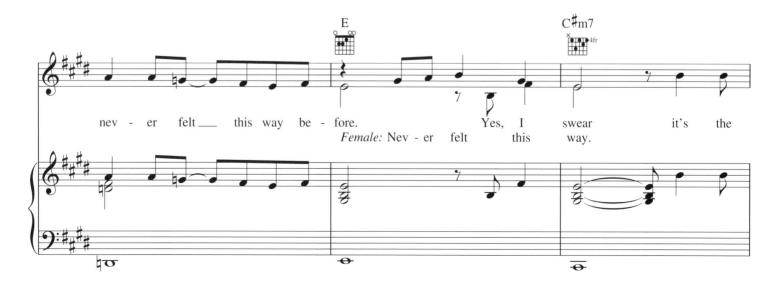

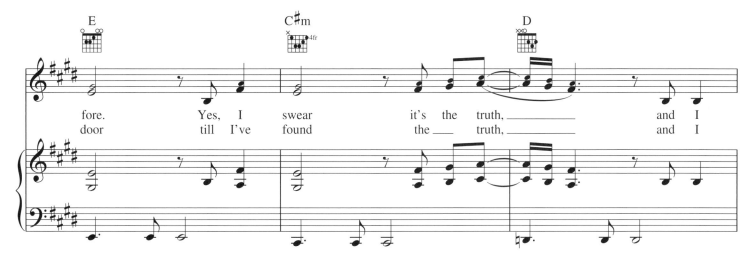

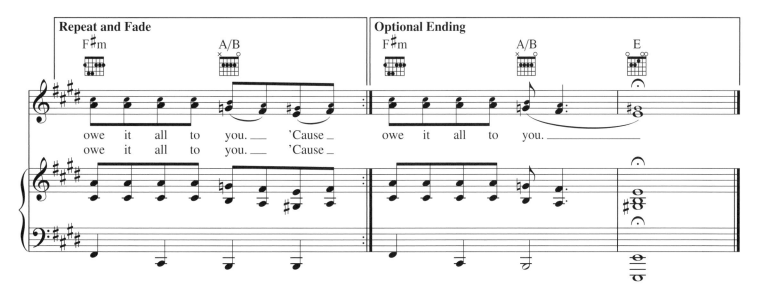

TRULY, MADLY, DEEPLY

Words and Music by DANIEL JONES
and DARREN HAYES

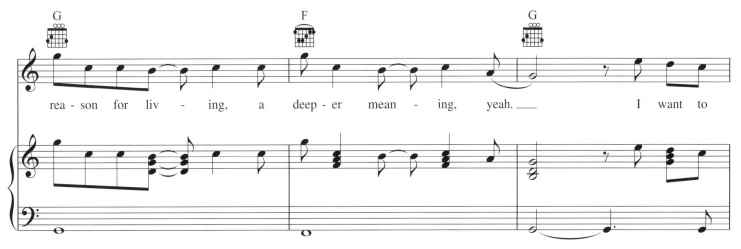

rea - son for liv - ing, a deep - er mean - ing, yeah.___ I want to

stand with you on a moun - tain, I want to bathe with you in the sea,___

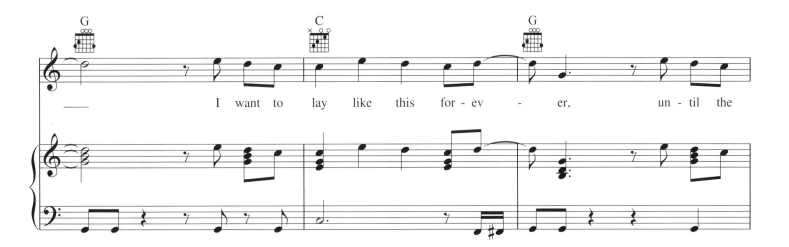

___ I want to lay like this for - ev - er, un - til the

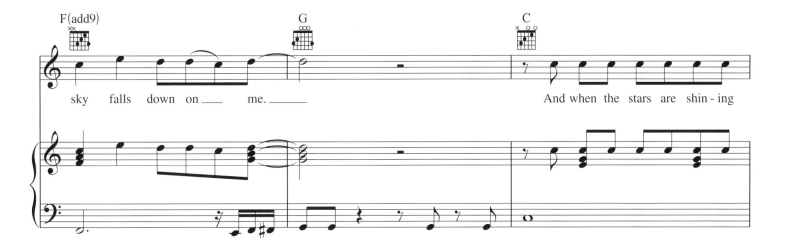

sky falls down on ___ me.___ And when the stars are shin - ing

bright-ly in the vel-vet sky, I'll make a wish, send it to heav-en, then make you want to cry __

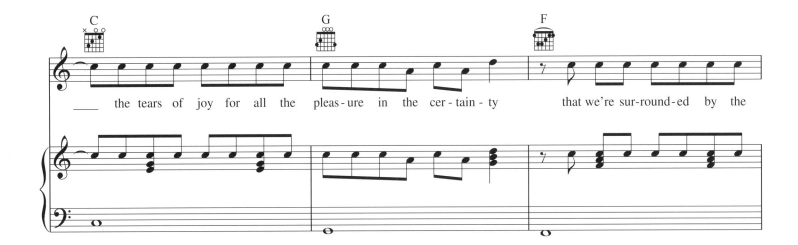

__ the tears of joy for all the pleas-ure in the cer-tain-ty that we're sur-round-ed by the

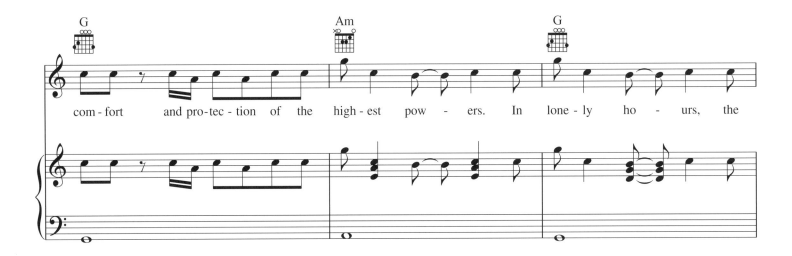

com-fort and pro-tec-tion of the high-est pow — ers. In lone-ly ho — urs, the

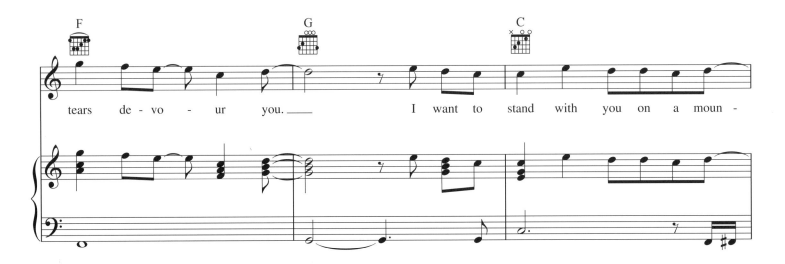

tears de-vo — ur you. __ I want to stand with you on a moun-

-tain, I want to bathe with you in the sea, _____ I want to

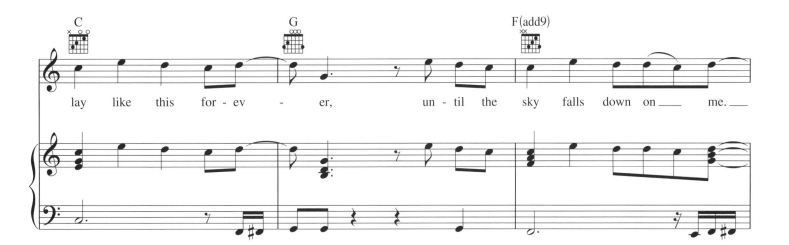

lay like this for-ev - er, un-til the sky falls down on ___ me. ___

___ Oh, can you see ___ it, ba - by?

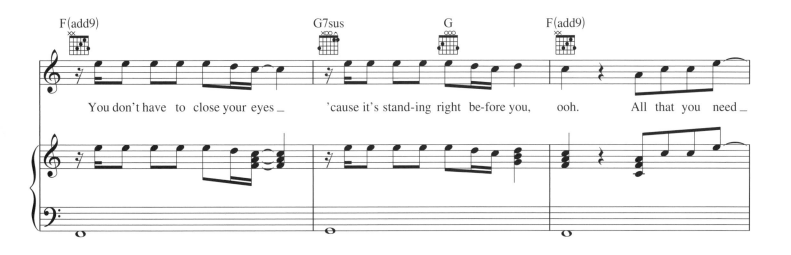

You don't have to close your eyes ___ 'cause it's stand-ing right be-fore you, ooh. All that you need ___

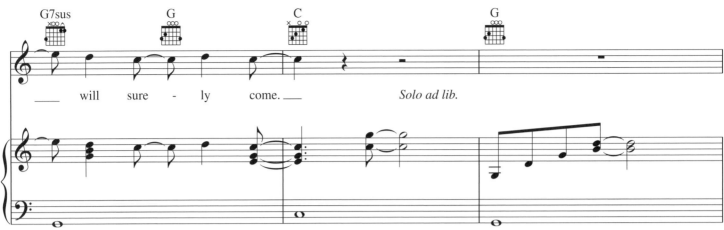

will sure - ly come. ___ *Solo ad lib.*

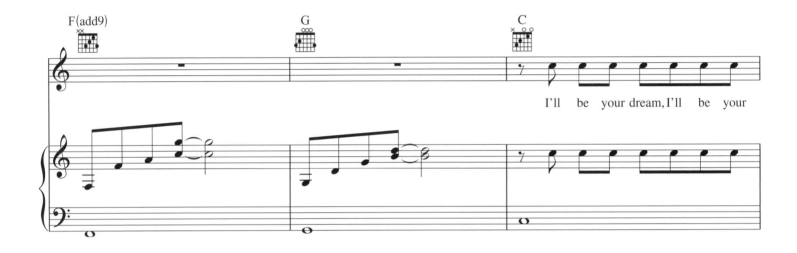

I'll be your dream, I'll be your

wish, I'll be your fan - ta - sy. I'll be your hope, I'll be your love, be ev - 'ry - thing that you need. ___

___ I'll love you more with ev - 'ry breath, tru - ly, mad - ly, deep - ly do. _____

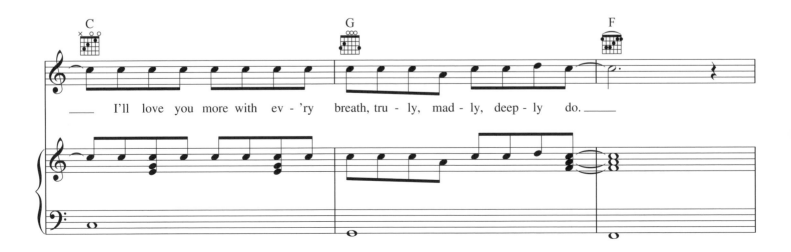

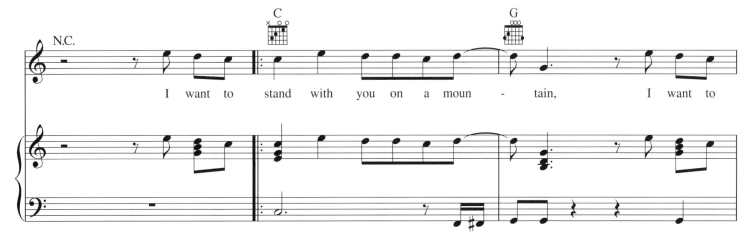

I want to stand with you on a moun - tain, I want to

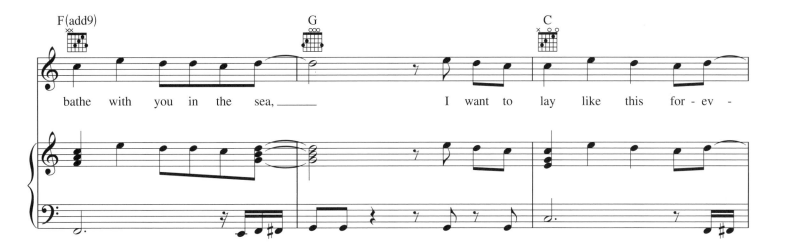

bathe with you in the sea, _____ I want to lay like this for - ev -

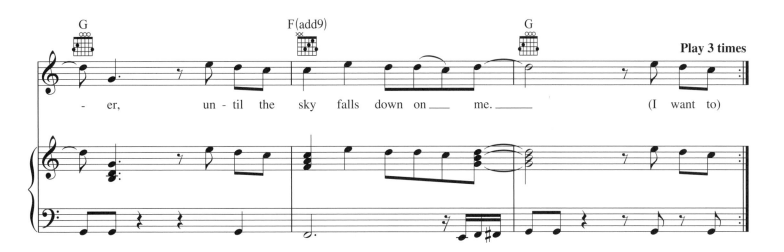

- er, un - til the sky falls down on ___ me. _____ (I want to)

Play 3 times

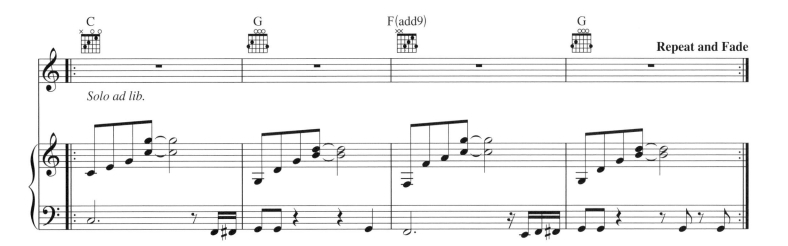

Solo ad lib.

Repeat and Fade

WHAT A WONDERFUL WORLD

Words and Music by GEORGE DAVID WEISS
and BOB THIELE

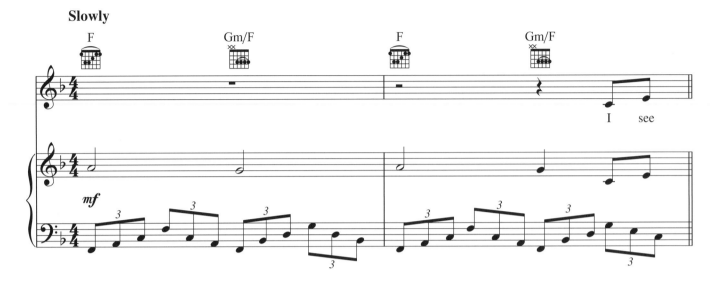

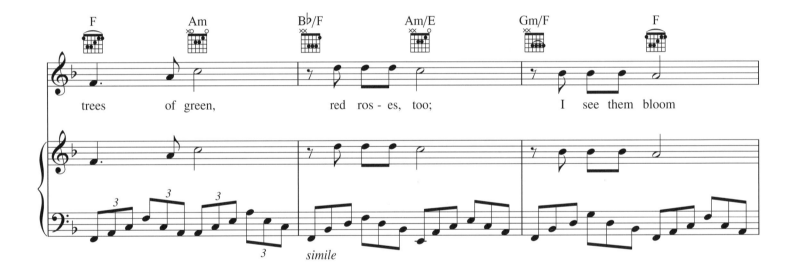

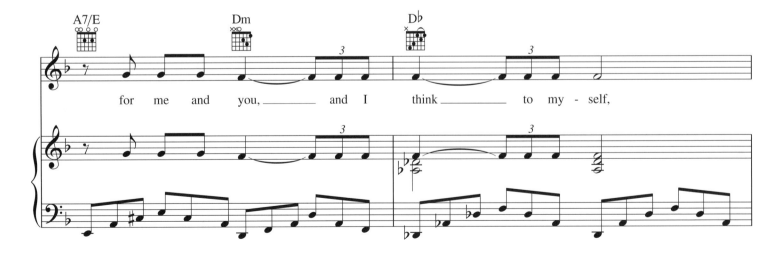

"What a won-der-ful world." _____ I see

skies of blue and clouds of white, the bright ___ bless-ed day, the

dark _____ sa-cred night, _____ and I think _____ to my-self,

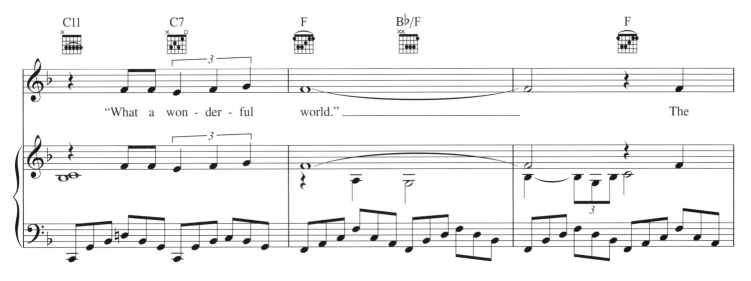

"What a won-der-ful world." _____ The

col - ors of the rain - bow, so pret - ty in the sky, are

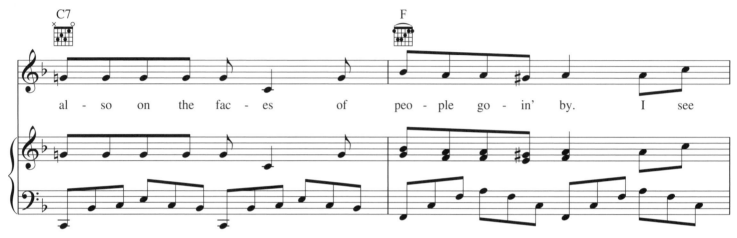

al - so on the fac - es of peo - ple go - in' by. I see

friends shak - in' hands, _____ say - in', "How do you do!"

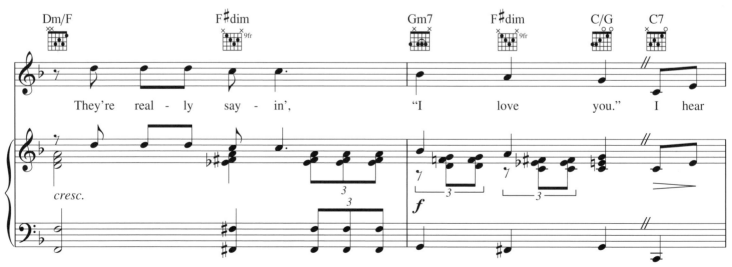

They're real - ly say - in', "I love you." I hear

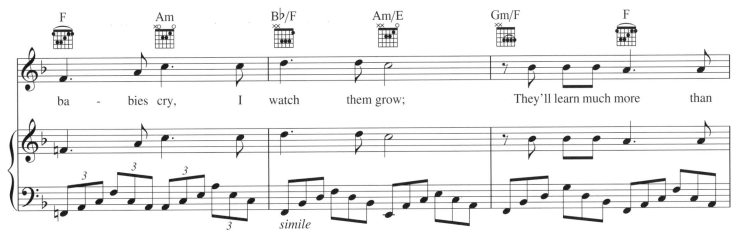

ba - bies cry, I watch them grow; They'll learn much more than

simile

I'll _____ ev-er know, ____ and I think _____ to my-self, "What a won-der-ful

Rubato

world." _____ Yes, I think to my-self,

"What a won-der-ful world." _____

rit.

YOU ARE THE SUNSHINE OF MY LIFE

Words and Music by
STEVIE WONDER

Moderately, with feeling

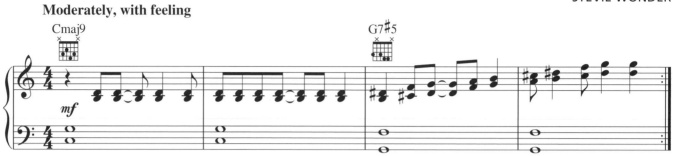

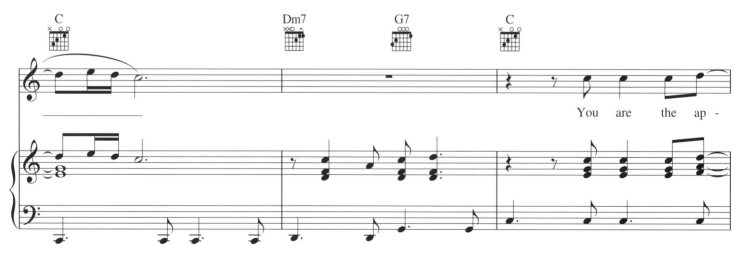

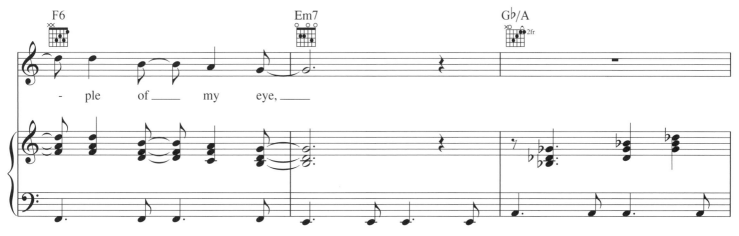

-ple of ____ my eye, ____

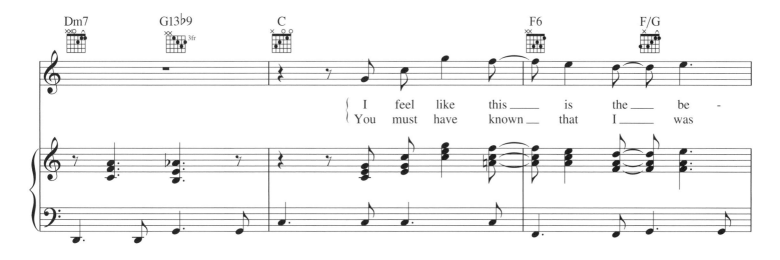

for - ev - er you'll ___ stay in ___ my heart. _____

I feel like this ____ is the ___ be -
You must have known ___ that I ____ was

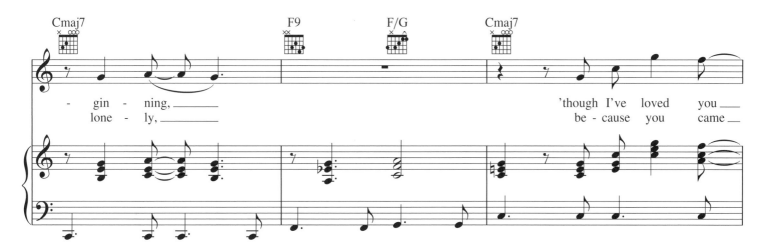

- gin - ning, _____
lone - ly, _____

'though I've loved you ___
be - cause you came ___

for a mil - lion years.
to my res - cue.

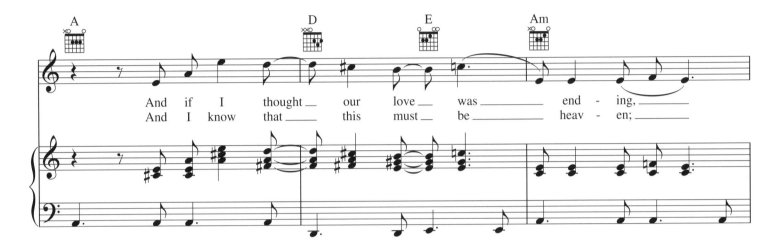

And if I thought our love was end - ing,
And I know that this must be heav - en;

I'd find my - self drown - ing in my own
how could so much love be in - side of

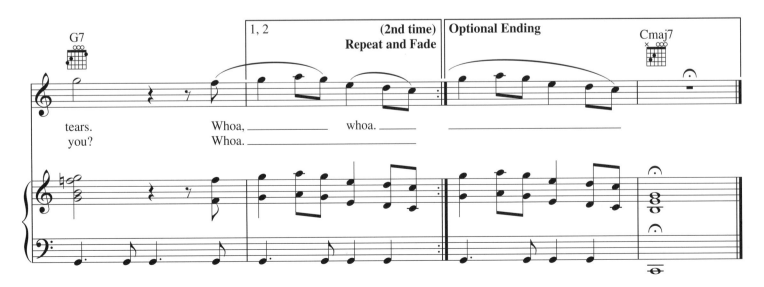

tears.
you?

Whoa, whoa.
Whoa.

YOU'RE THE INSPIRATION

Words and Music by PETER CETERA
and DAVID FOSTER

Rock Ballad

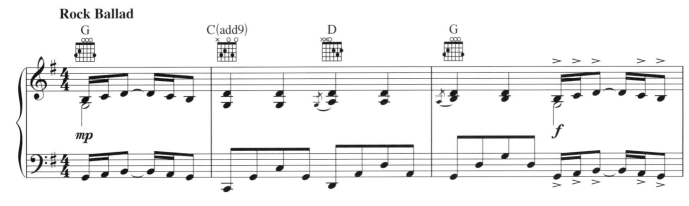

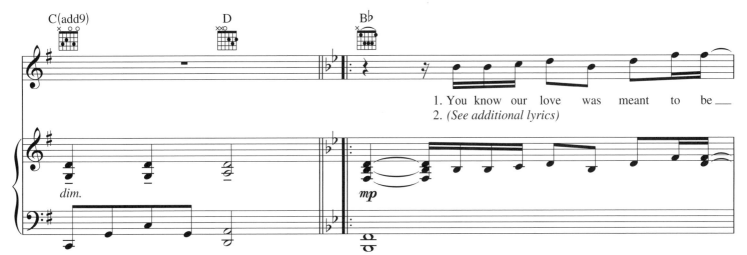

1. You know our love was meant to be ___
2. *(See additional lyrics)*

the kind of love ___ that lasts ___ for -

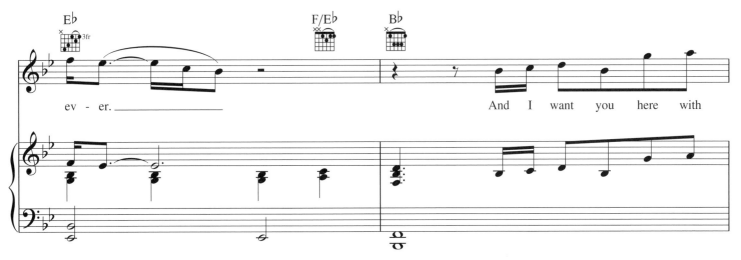

ev - er. _____ And I want you here with

You bring feel-ing to my life, ___ you're the in-spi-ra - tion.

Wan-na have you near me, I wan-na have you hear me say-ing ___

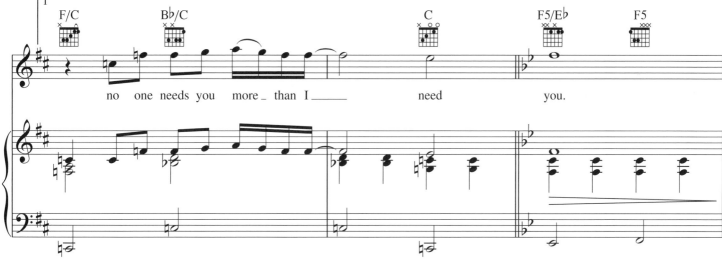

no one needs you more_ than I ___ need you.

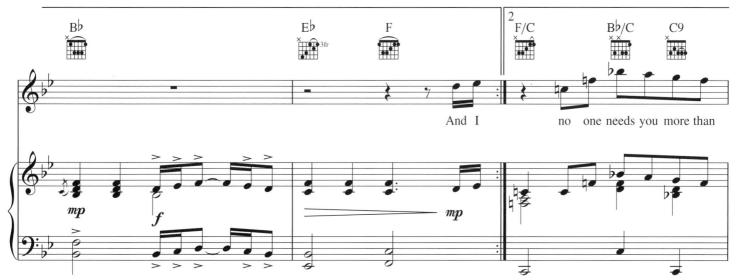

And I no one needs you more than

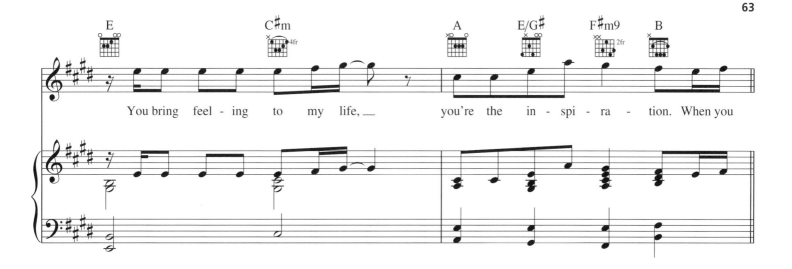

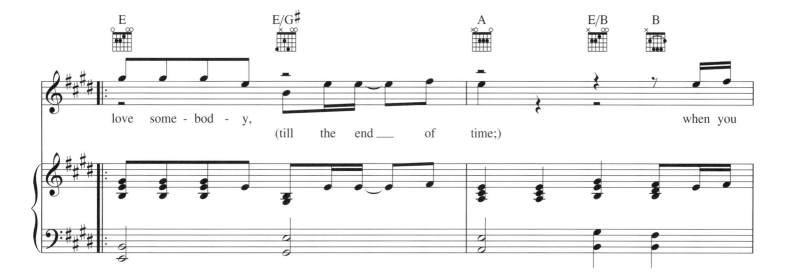

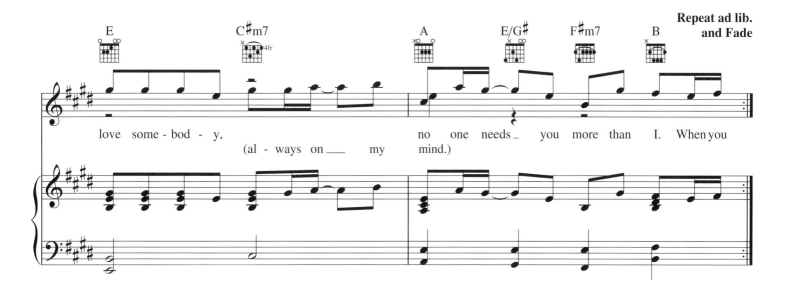

Additional Lyrics

2. And I know (yes, I know)
That it's plain to see
We're so in love when we're together.
Now I know (now I know)
That I need you here with me
From tonight until the end of time.
You should know everywhere I go;
Always on my mind, you're in my heart, in my soul.
Chorus

BEAUTIFUL IN MY EYES

Words and Music by
JOSHUA KADISON

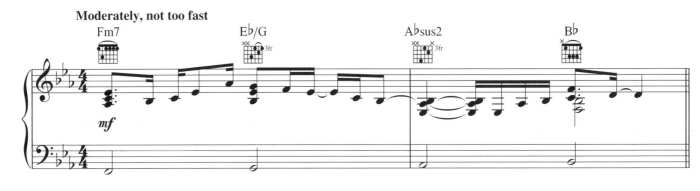

You're my peace of mind ___ in this
The world ___ will turn ___ and the
lines up- on ___ my face ___ from a

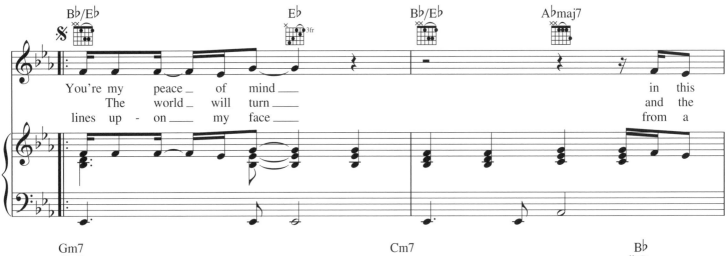

cra - zy world. ___ You're ev- 'ry- thing I've
sea - sons will change, and all the les - sons
life - time of smiles, when the time comes

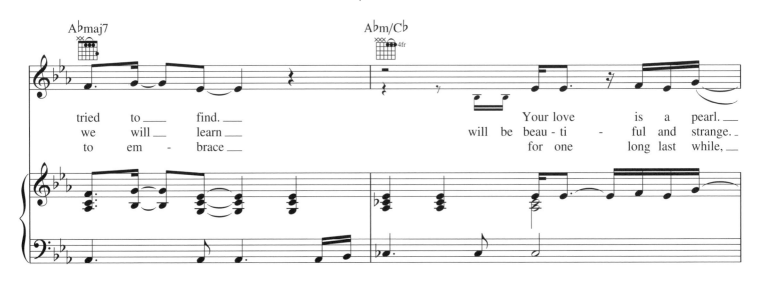

tried to ___ find. ___ Your love is a pearl.
we will ___ learn will be beau- ti - ful and strange. ___
to em - brace ___ for one long last while, ___

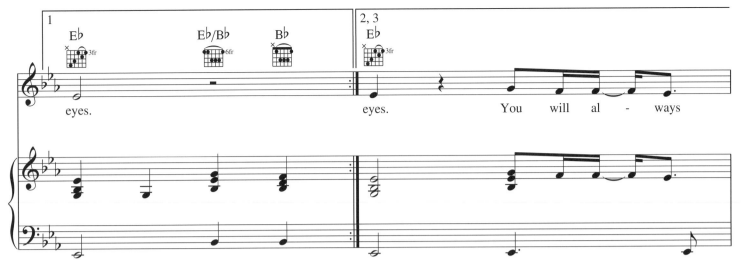

eyes.   eyes.   You will al - ways

be   beau - ti - ful in my eyes. ___

And the pass - ing years ___ will show ___ that you will al - ways

grow ___ ev - er more ___ beau - ti - ful ___ in my

D.S. al Coda
(take 2nd ending)

eyes.   When there are

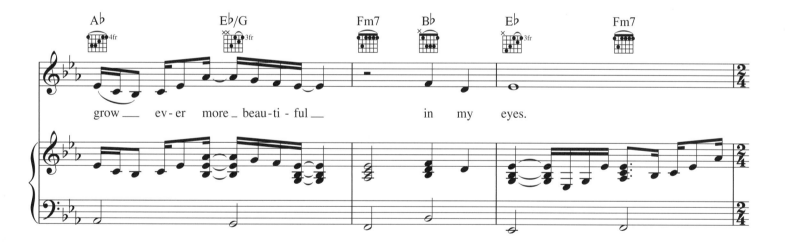

eyes.   The pass - ing years __ will   show __   that you   will al - ways

grow __ ev - er   more __ beau-ti - ful __   in   my   eyes.

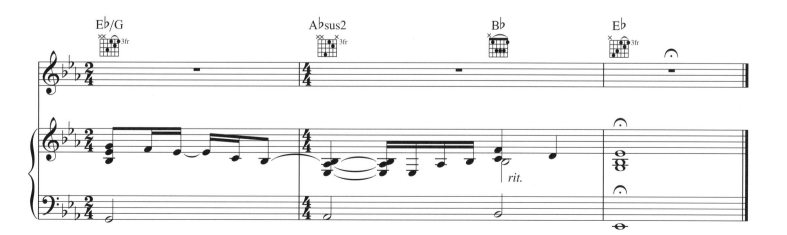

rit.

FROM THIS MOMENT ON

Words and Music by SHANIA TWAIN
and R.J. LANGE

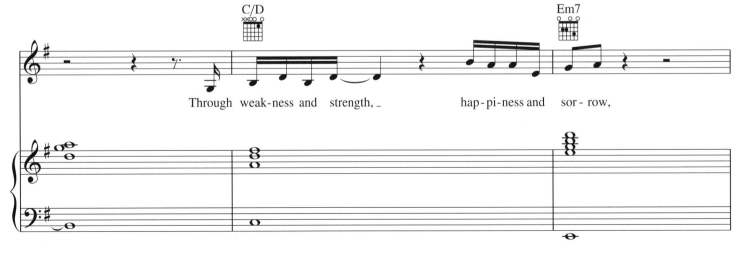

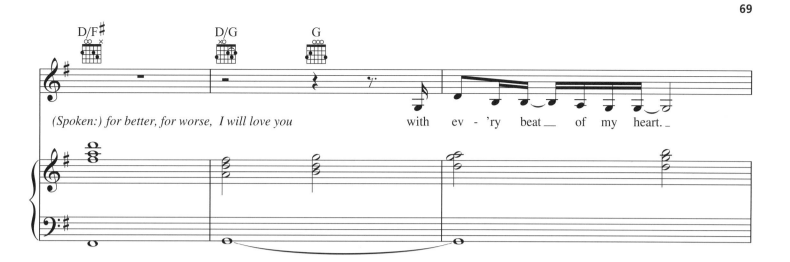

(Spoken:) for better, for worse, I will love you with ev - 'ry beat __ of my heart. __

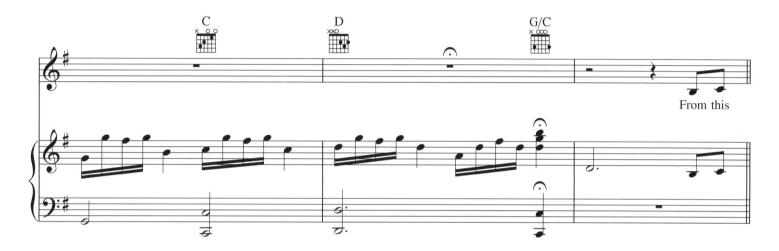

From this

Slowly

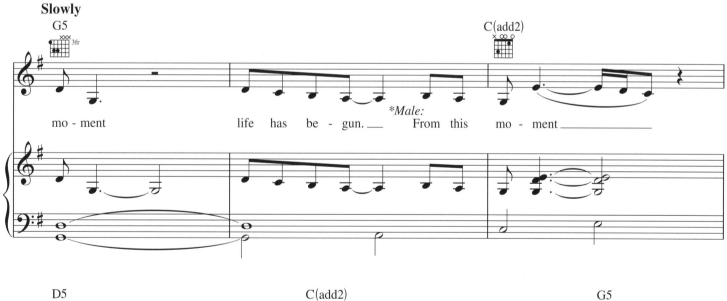

mo - ment ____ life has be - gun. __ *Male:* From this mo - ment __

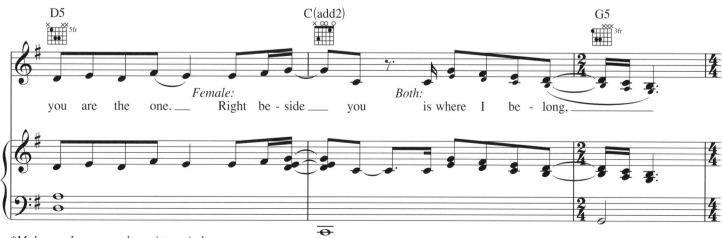

you are the one. __ *Female:* Right be - side __ you *Both:* is where I be - long, __

Male vocals sung at the written pitch.

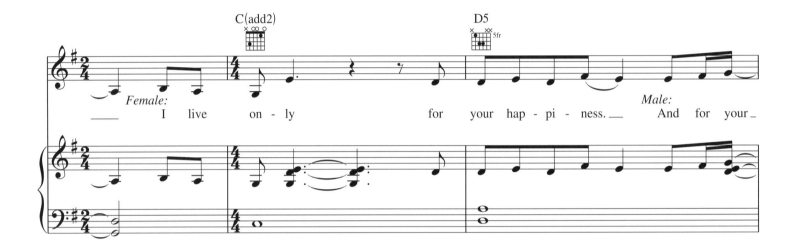

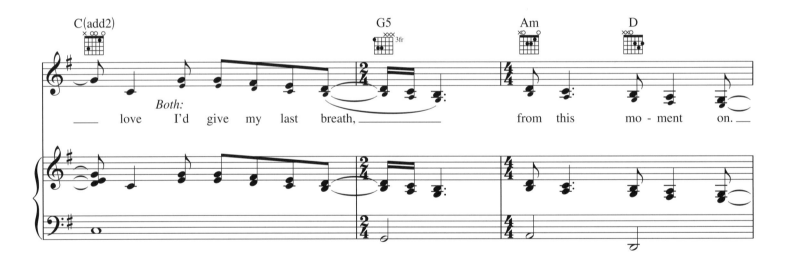

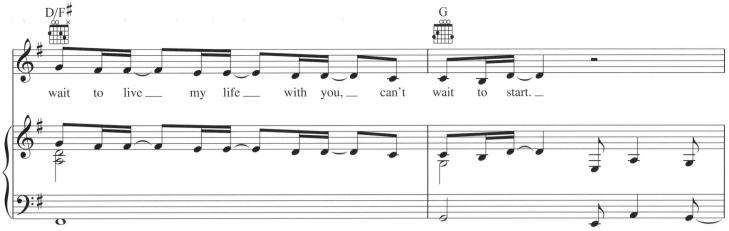

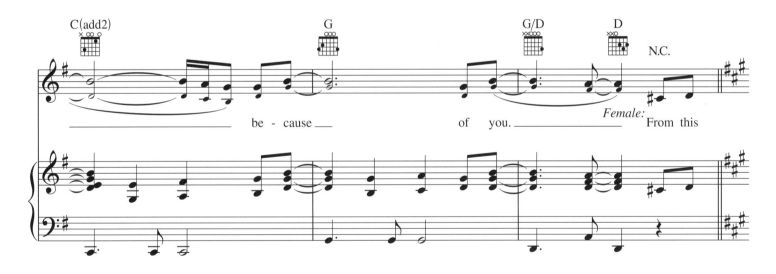

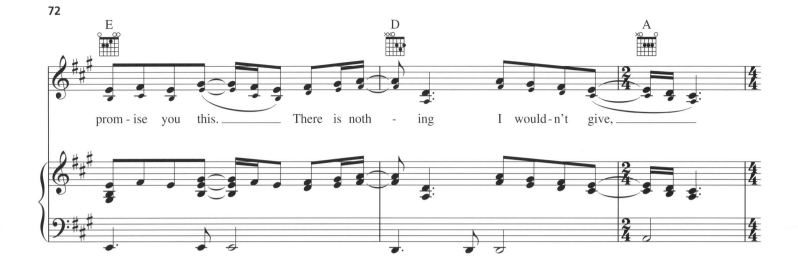

prom-ise you this. _____ There is noth - ing I would-n't give, _____

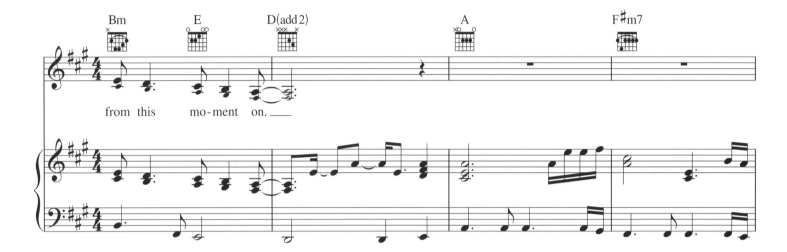

from this mo-ment on. ____

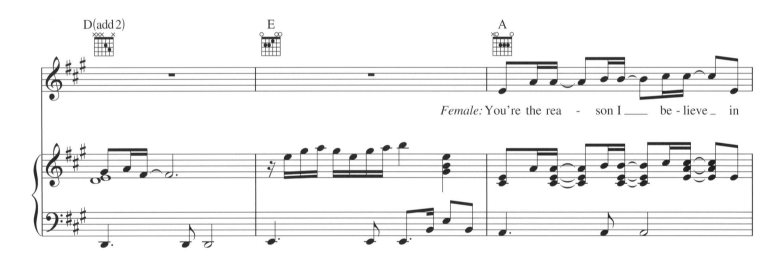

Female: You're the rea - son I ___ be - lieve _ in

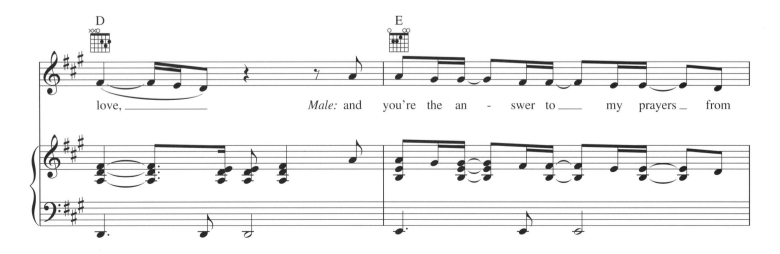

love, _____ *Male:* and you're the an - swer to ___ my prayers _ from

up a - bove. _____ *Both:* All we need _____ is just _____ the two _____ of

us. _____ My dreams _____ came true _____ be - cause _

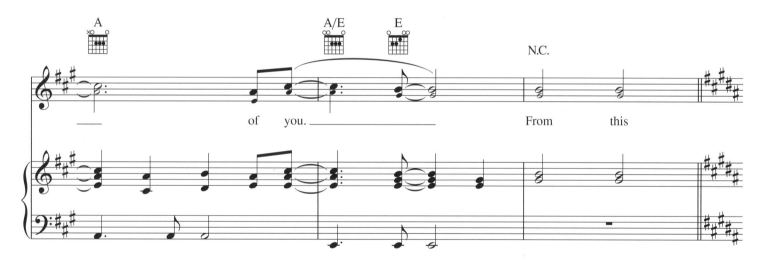

_____ of you. _____ From this

mo - ment, as long as I live, _____ I _____ will

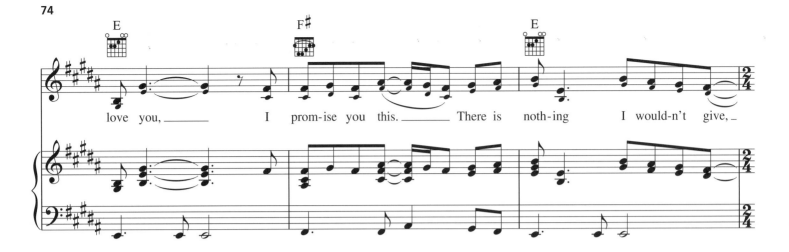

love you, _____ I prom-ise you this. _____ There is noth-ing I would-n't give, _

_____ from this mo-ment. I will love _____ you, I will love _____ you _ as

Female: *Male:* *Female:*

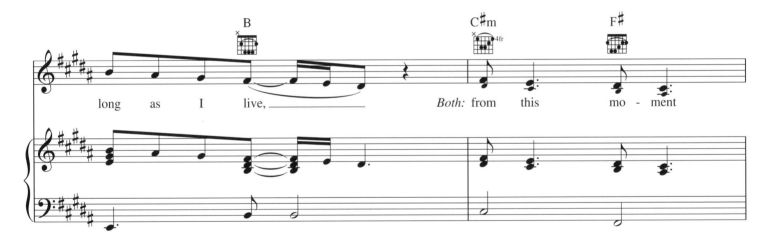

long as I live, _____ *Both:* from this mo - ment

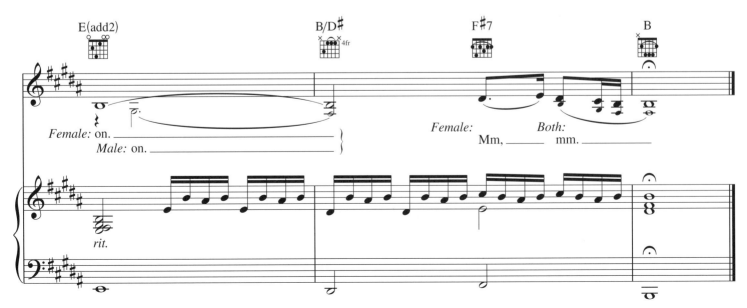

Female: on. _____
Male: on. _____

Female: *Both:*
Mm, _____ mm. _____

rit.

COULD I HAVE THIS DANCE

from URBAN COWBOY

Words and Music by WAYLAND HOLYFIELD
and BOB HOUSE

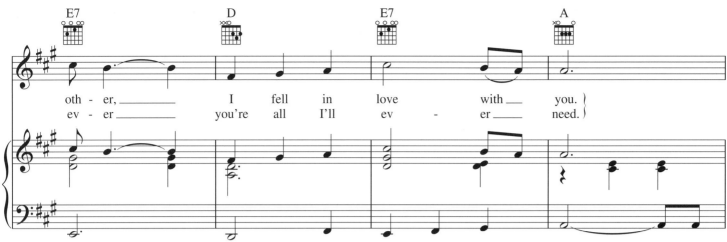

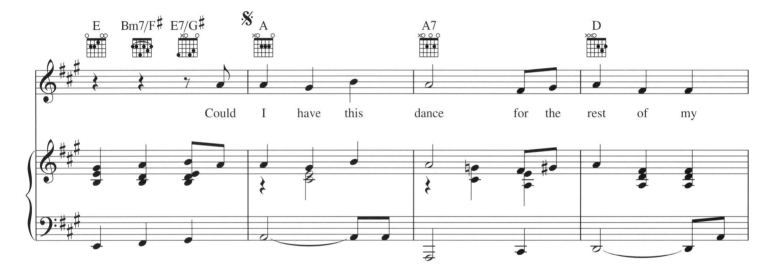

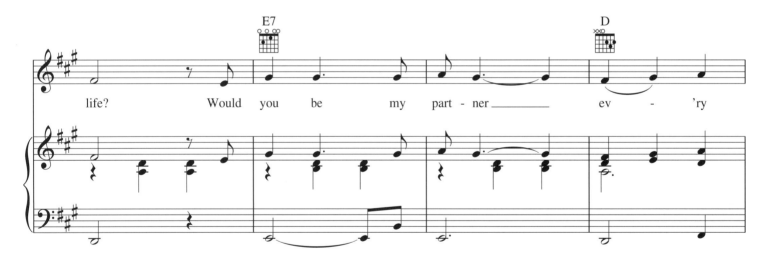

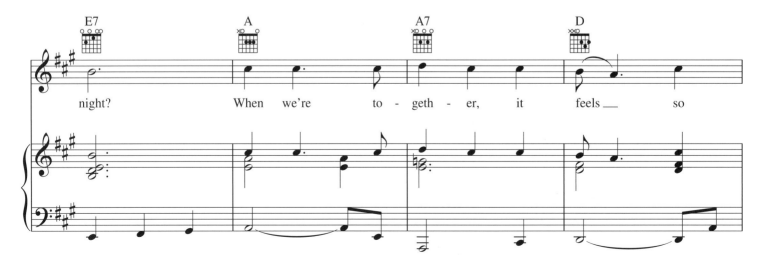

right. ___ Could I have ___ this dance for the rest of my ___

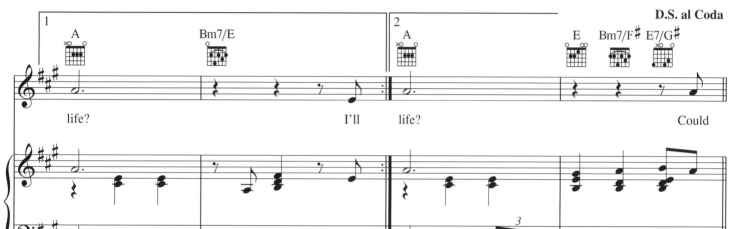

life? I'll life? Could

rest of my ___ life? ___

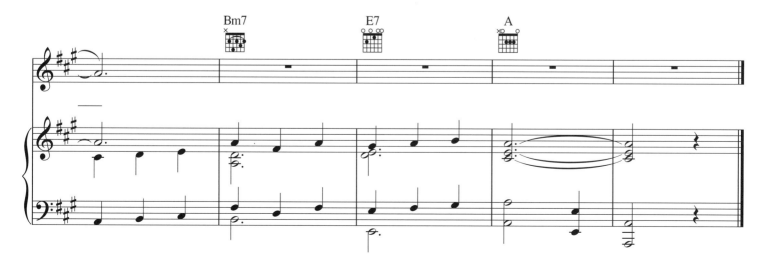

WONDERFUL TONIGHT

Words and Music by
ERIC CLAPTON

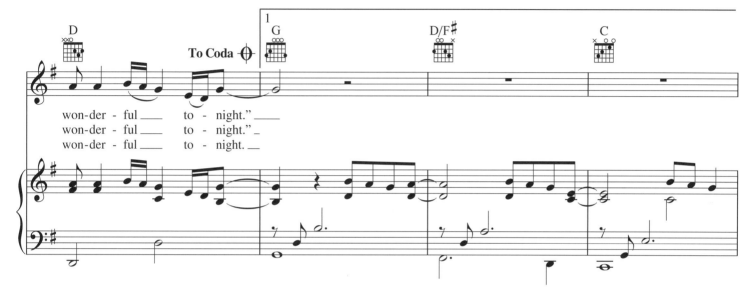

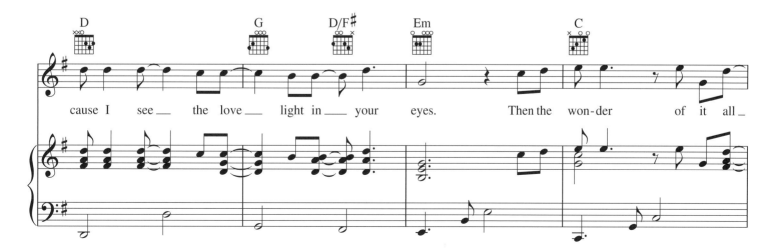

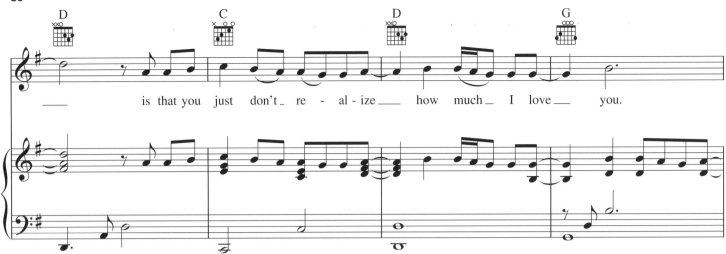

is that you just don't re - al - ize ___ how much ___ I love ___ you.

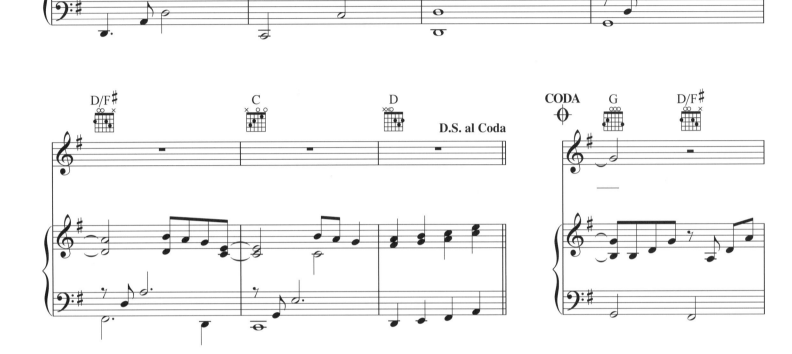

D.S. al Coda

CODA

Oh, my dar-ling, you are won-der-ful ___ to - night." ___

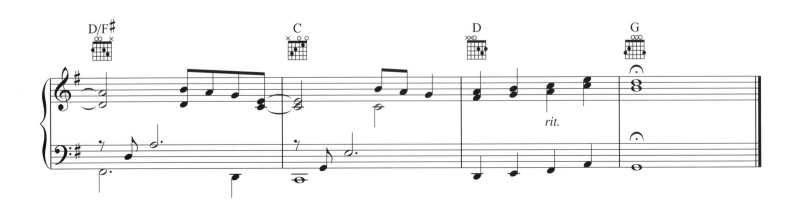

rit.

TODAY WAS A FAIRYTALE

from VALENTINE'S DAY

Words and Music by
TAYLOR SWIFT

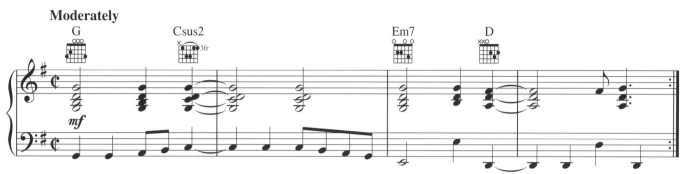

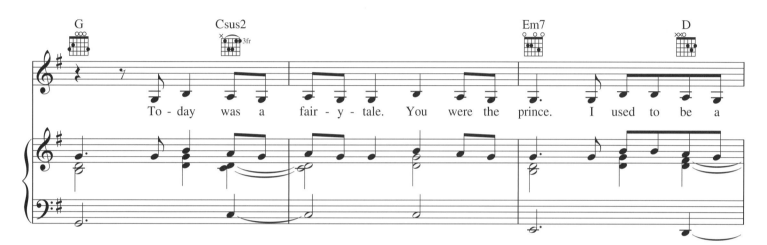

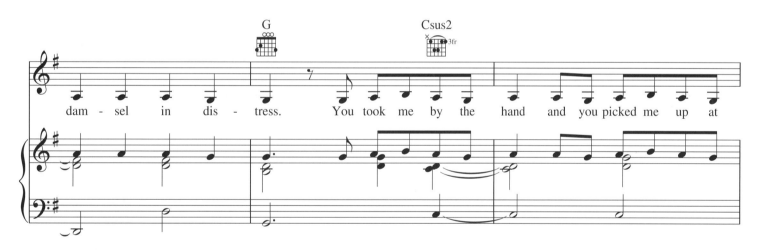

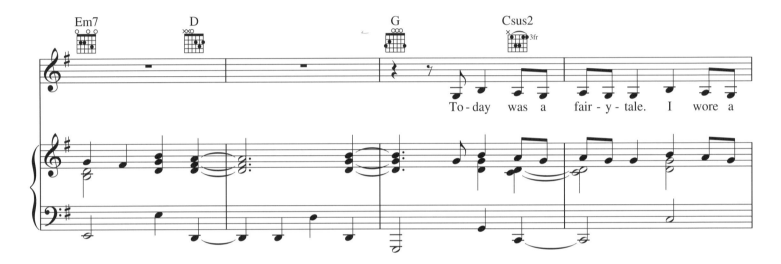

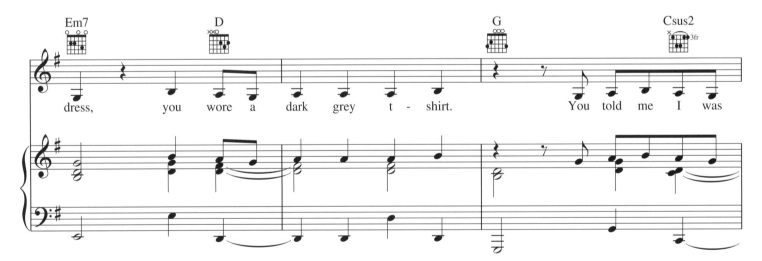

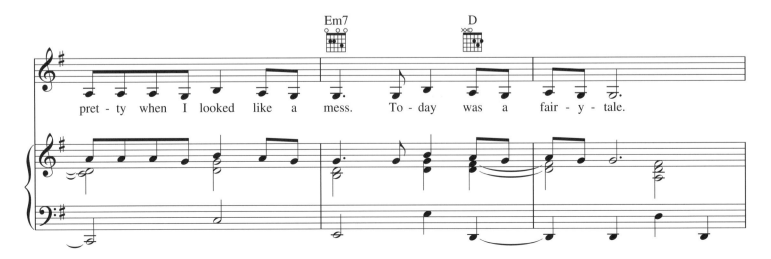

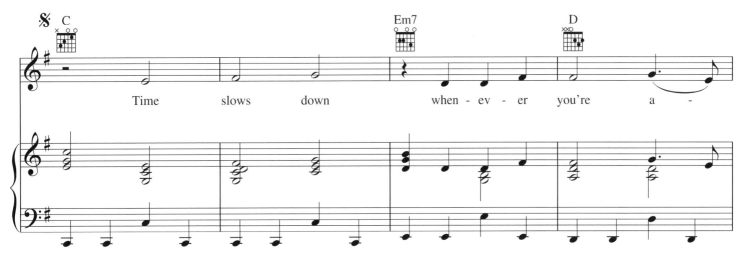

Time slows down when - ev - er you're a -

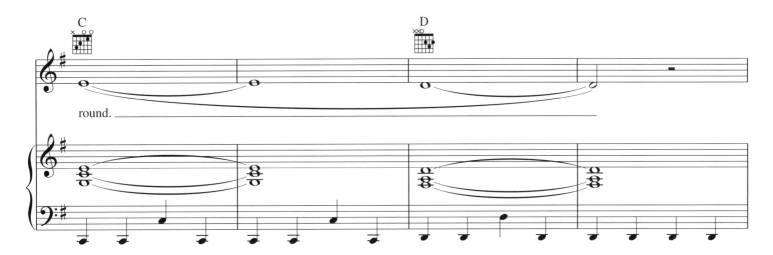

round. _____

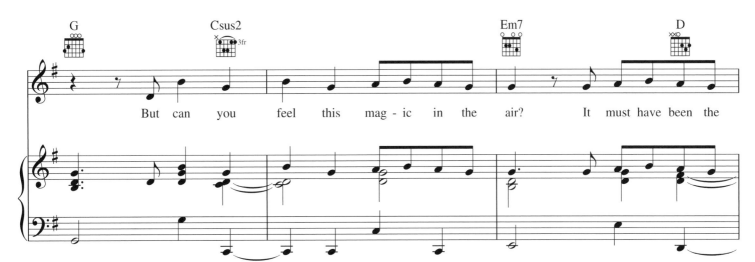

But can you feel this mag - ic in the air? It must have been the

way you kissed me. _____ Fell in love when I saw you stand - in'

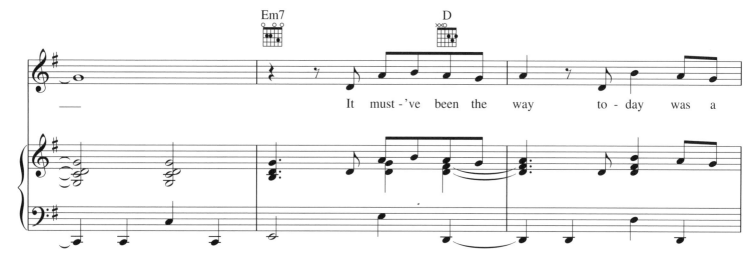

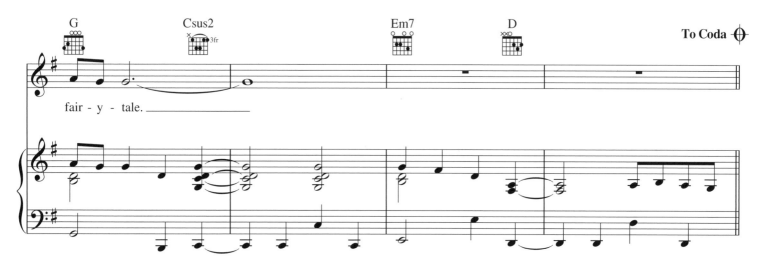

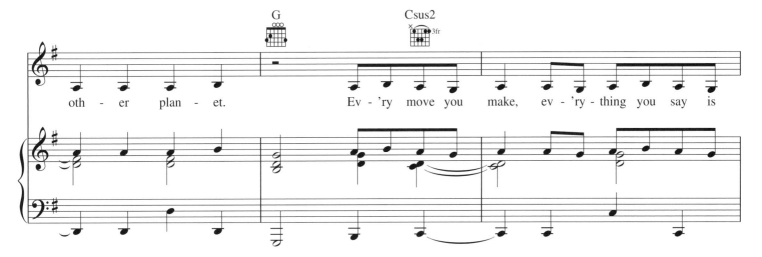

oth - er plan - et. Ev - 'ry move you make, ev - 'ry-thing you say is

right. To - day was a fair - y - tale. To - day was a

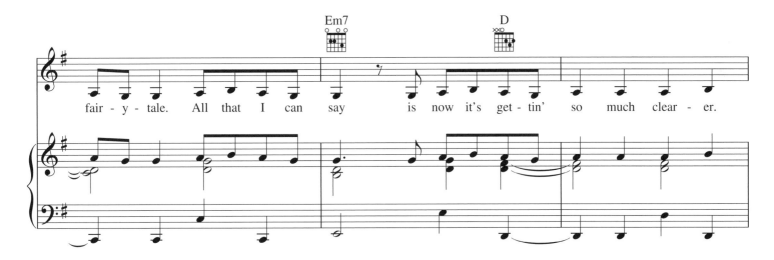

fair - y - tale. All that I can say is now it's get - tin' so much clear - er.

D.S. al Coda

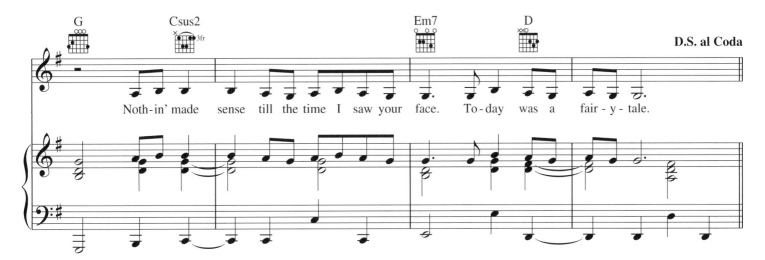

Noth-in' made sense till the time I saw your face. To - day was a fair - y - tale.

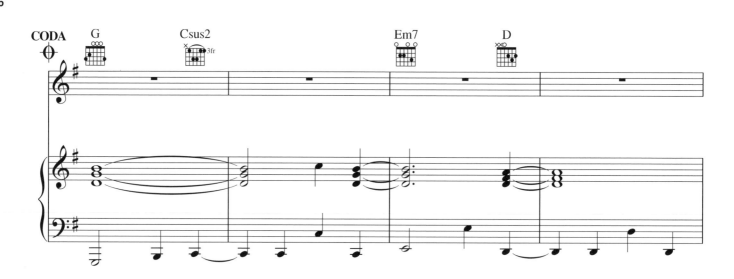

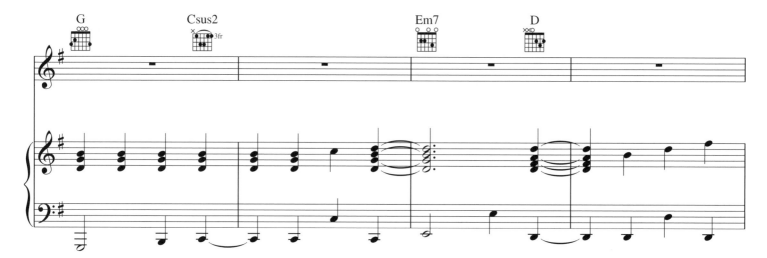

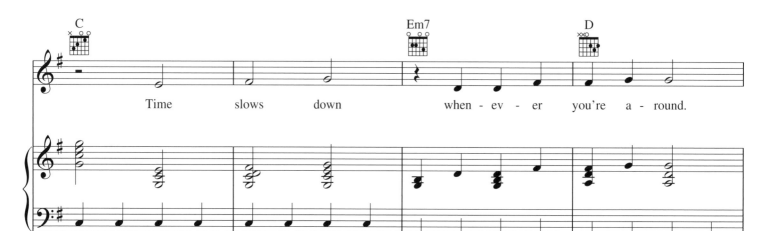

Time slows down when-ev-er you're a-round.

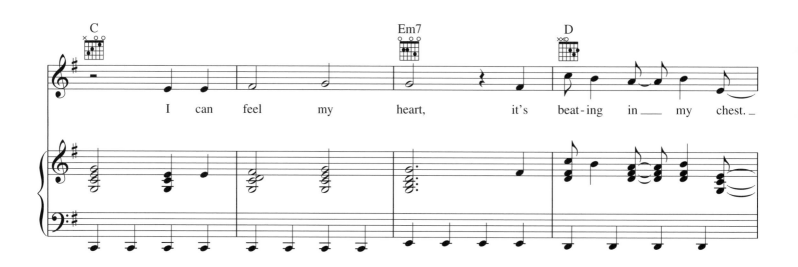

I can feel my heart, it's beat-ing in ___ my chest. ___

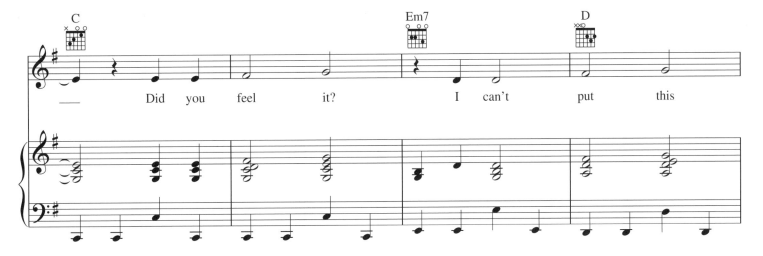

Did you feel it? I can't put this

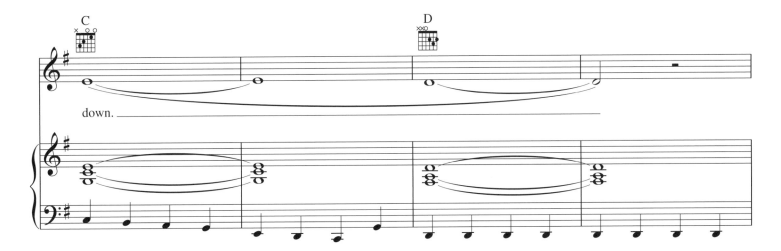

down. _____

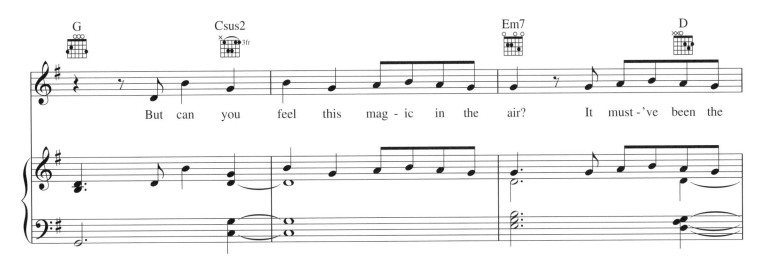

But can you feel this mag - ic in the air? It must - 've been the

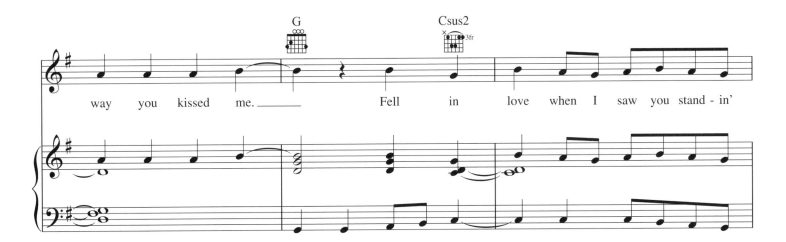

way you kissed me. _____ Fell in love when I saw you stand - in'

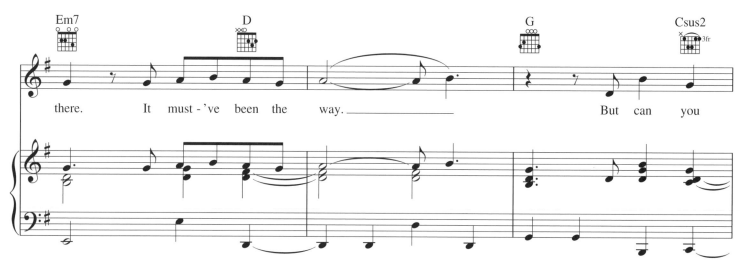

there. It must-'ve been the way._____ But can you

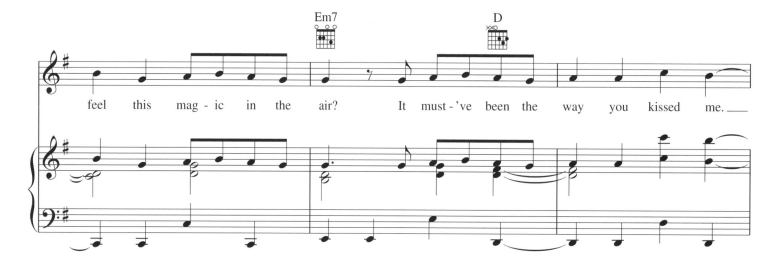

feel this mag-ic in the air? It must-'ve been the way you kissed me.___

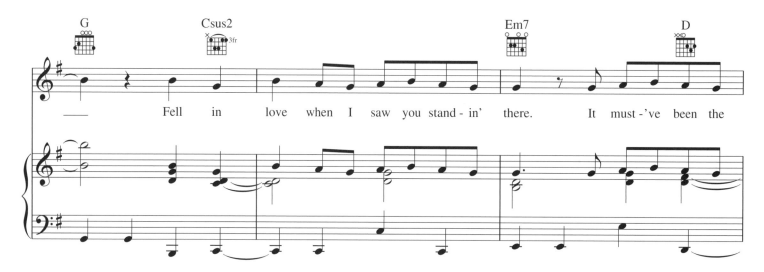

___ Fell in love when I saw you stand-in' there. It must-'ve been the

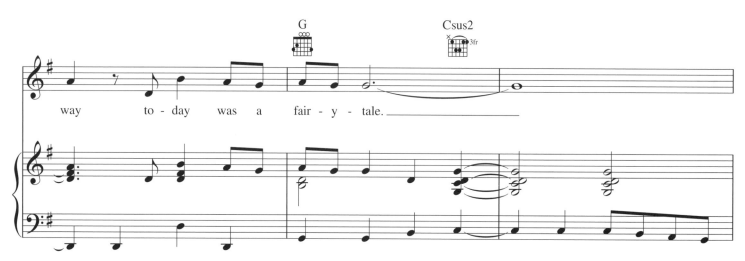

way to-day was a fair-y-tale._____

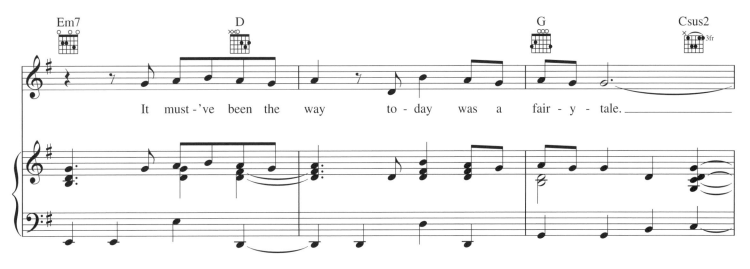

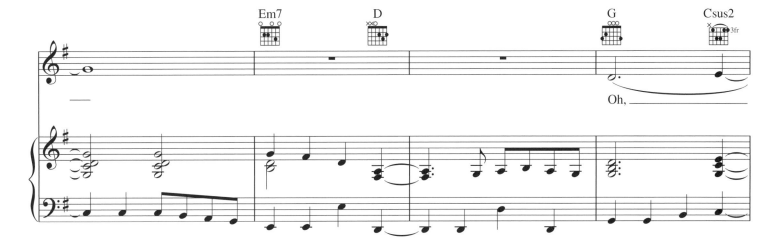

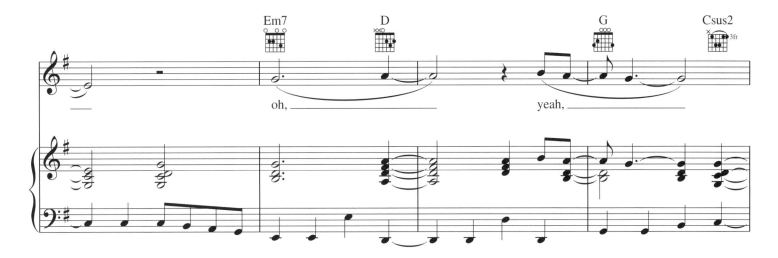

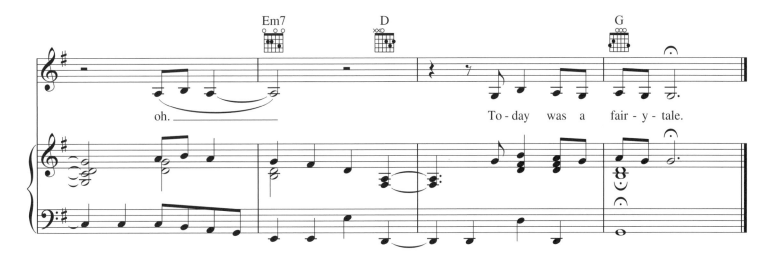

CINDERELLA

Words and Music by
STEVEN CURTIS CHAPMAN

With a lilt

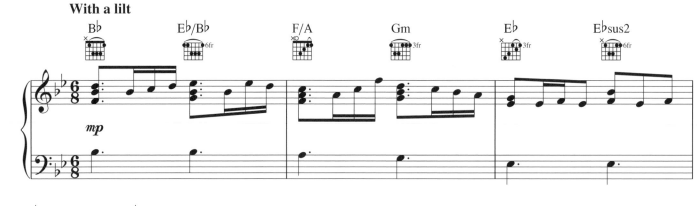

She spins and she sways __ to what-ev-er song plays,

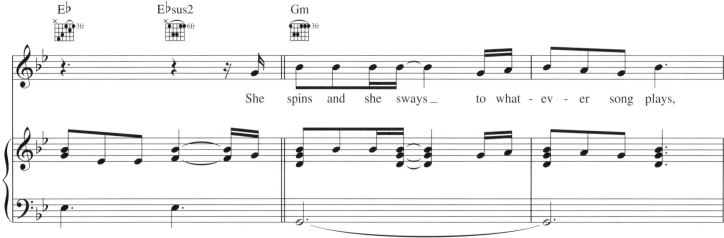

with-out a care __ in the world. __ And I'm sit-ting here wear-ing the

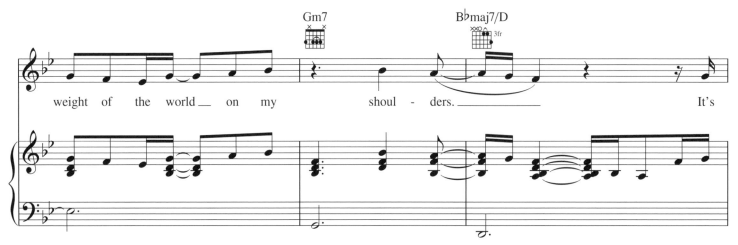

weight of the world __ on my shoul-ders. _____ It's

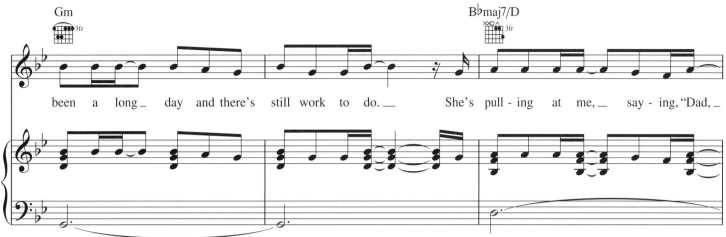

been a long _ day and there's still work to do. _ She's pull-ing at me, _ say-ing, "Dad, _

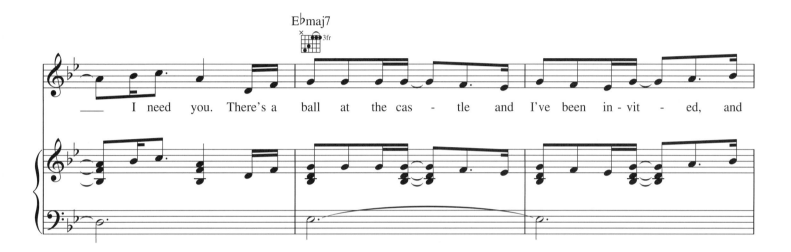

_ I need you. There's a ball at the cas-tle and I've been in-vit-ed, and

I need to prac-tice my danc-ing. Oh please, Dad-dy, please." _

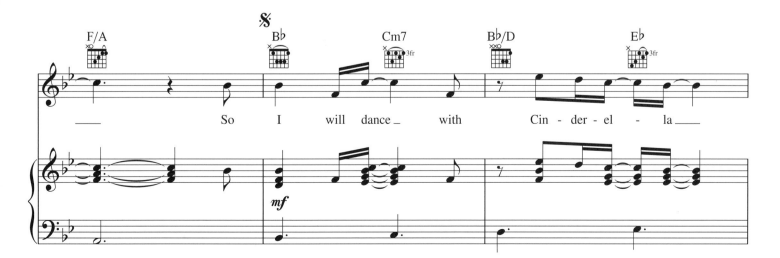

So I will dance _ with Cin-der-el-la _

while she is here ___ in my arms. ___ 'Cause I know

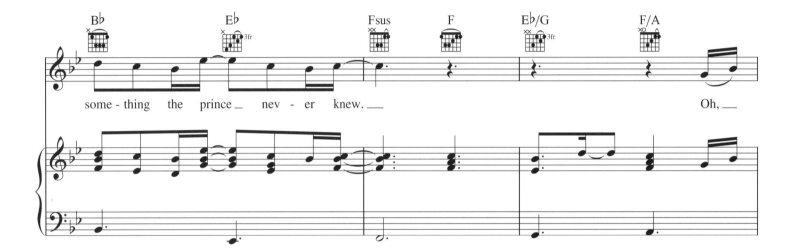

some - thing the prince ___ nev - er knew. ___ Oh, ___

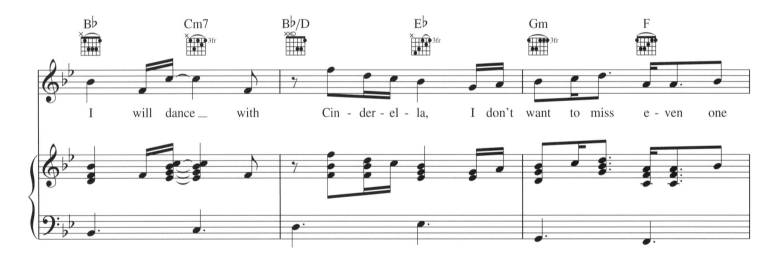

I will dance ___ with Cin - der - el - la, I don't want to miss e - ven one

song. 'Cause all too ___ soon, the clock will strike ___

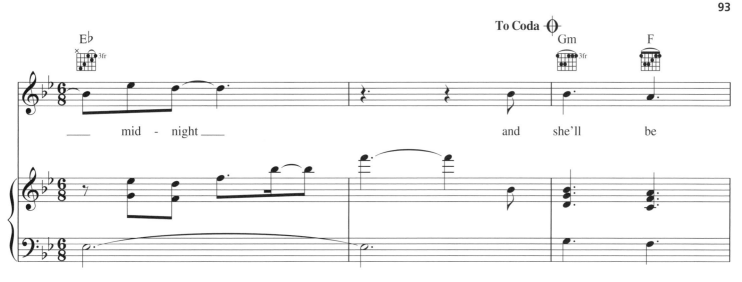

mid - night ___ and she'll be

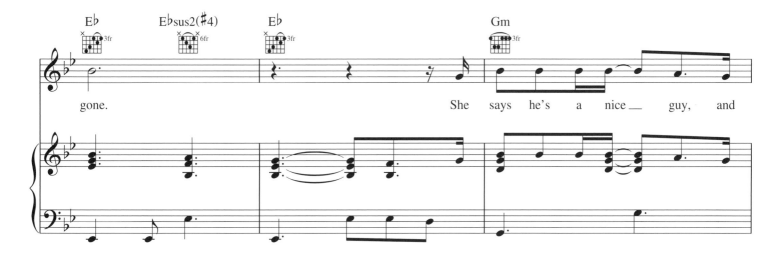

gone. She says he's a nice ___ guy, and

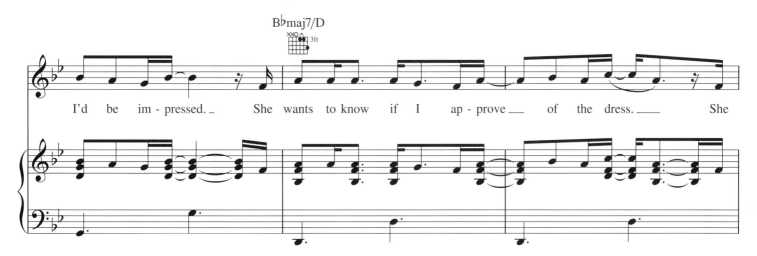

I'd be im - pressed. ___ She wants to know if I ap - prove ___ of the dress. ___ She

says, "Dad, the prom is just one week a - way ___ and I need to prac - tice my

D.S. al Coda

danc - ing. Oh please, Dad - dy, please." __ So

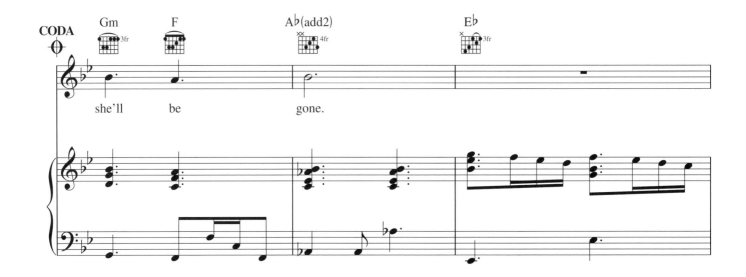

CODA

she'll be gone.

She will __ be gone. _____

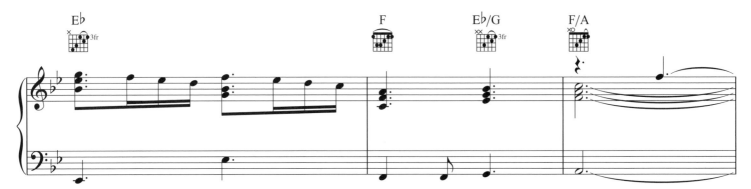

Well, she came home to - day _____ with a

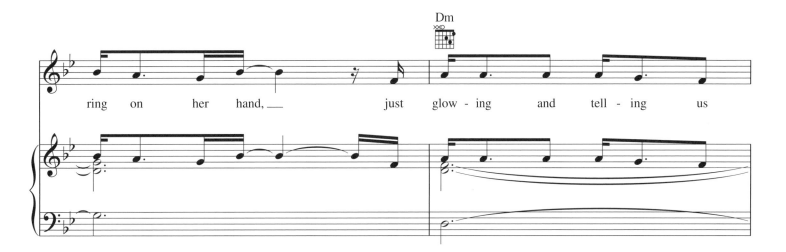

ring on her hand, ___ just glow - ing and tell - ing us

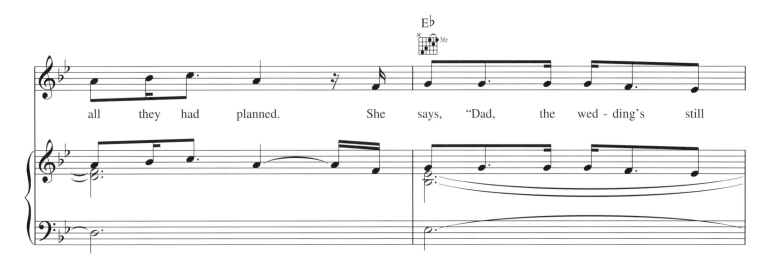

all they had planned. She says, "Dad, the wed - ding's still

six months a - way, ___ but I need to prac - tice my

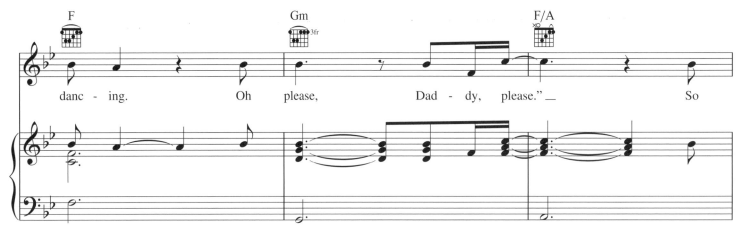

danc - ing. Oh please, Dad - dy, please." __ So

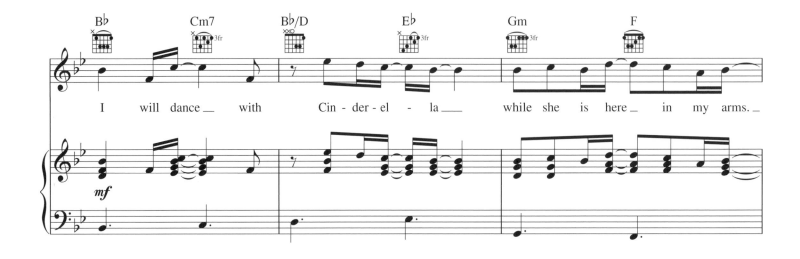

I will dance __ with Cin - der - el - la __ while she is here __ in my arms. __

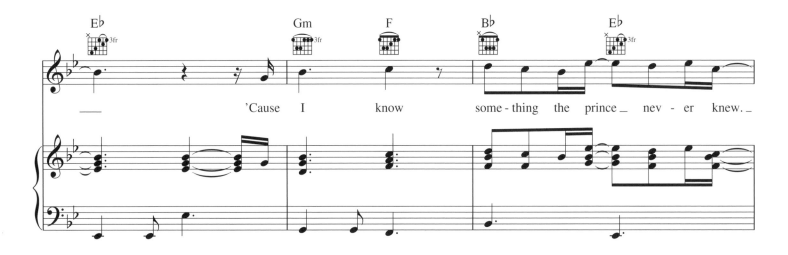

__ 'Cause I know some - thing the prince __ nev - er knew. __

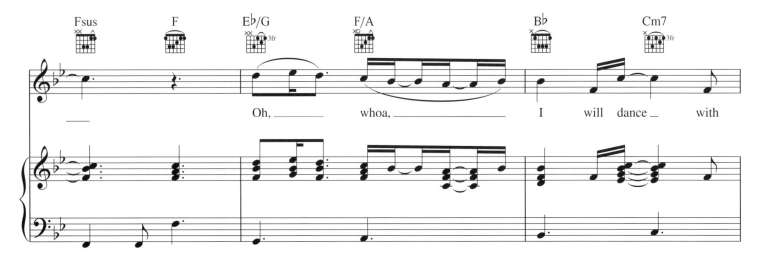

Oh, _____ whoa, _____ I will dance __ with

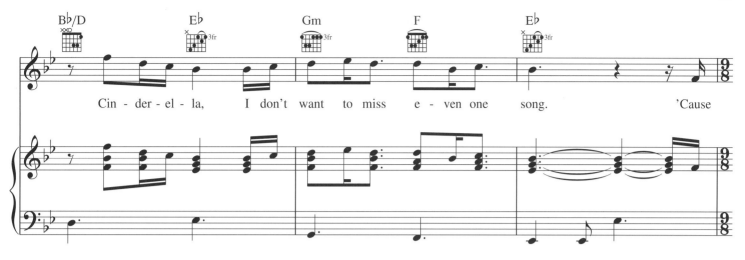

Cin - der - el - la, I don't want to miss e - ven one song. 'Cause

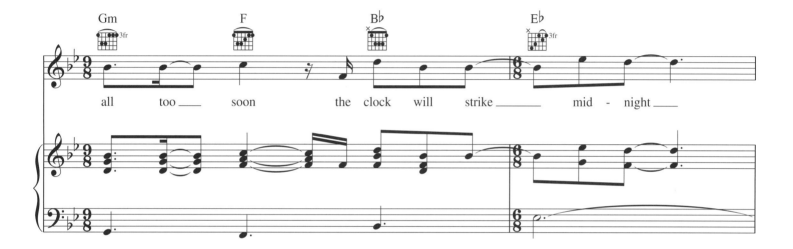

all too ___ soon the clock will strike ___ mid - night ___

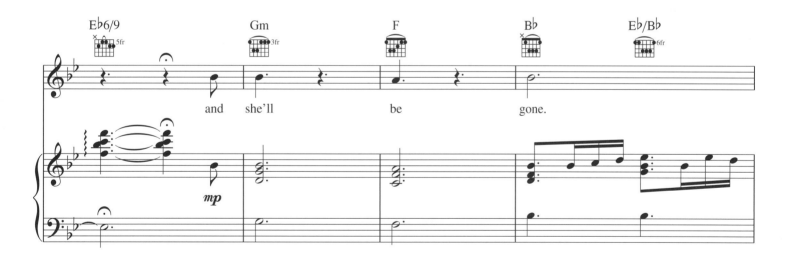

and she'll be gone.

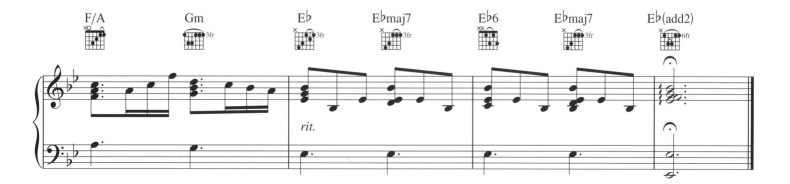

rit.

DADDY'S LITTLE GIRL

Words and Music by BOBBY BURKE
and HORACE GERLACH

Lit - tle girl of mine, with eyes of shin - ing

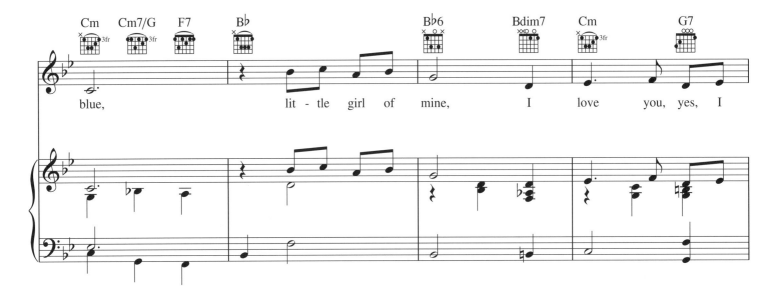

blue, lit - tle girl of mine, I love you, yes, I

do. No one else could be so sweet._____

You have made my life com - plete._____

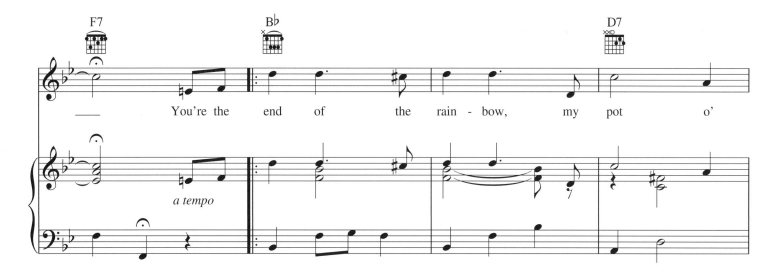

_____ You're the end of the rain - bow, my pot o'

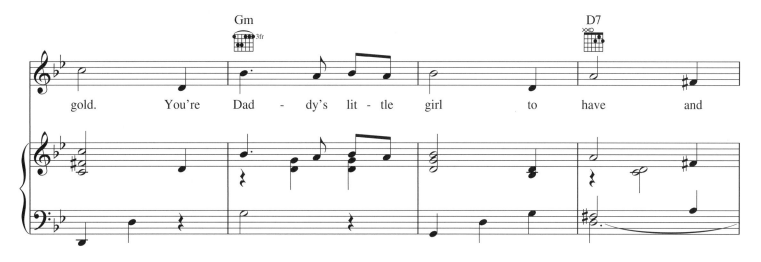

gold. You're Dad - dy's lit - tle girl to have and

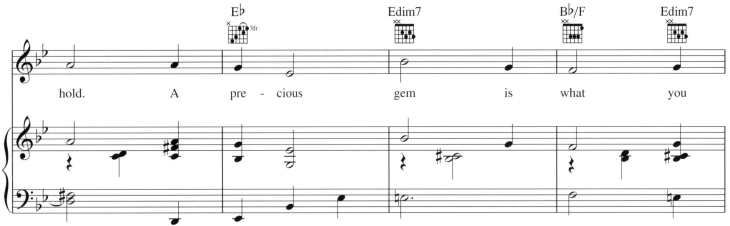

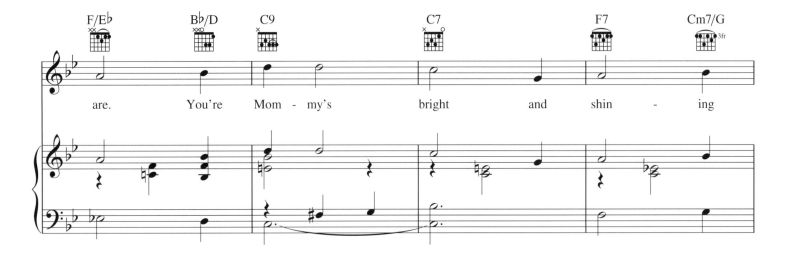

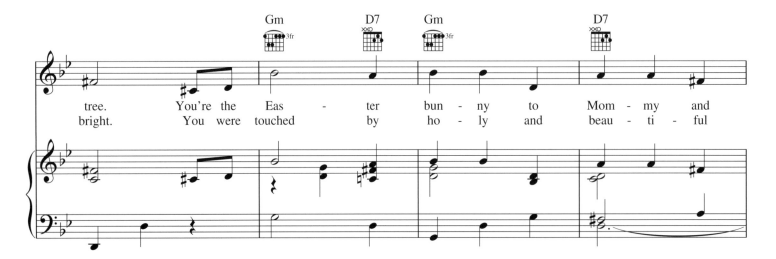

me. You're sug - ar. You're spice. You're ev - 'ry - thing
light. Like an - gels that sing, a heav - en - ly

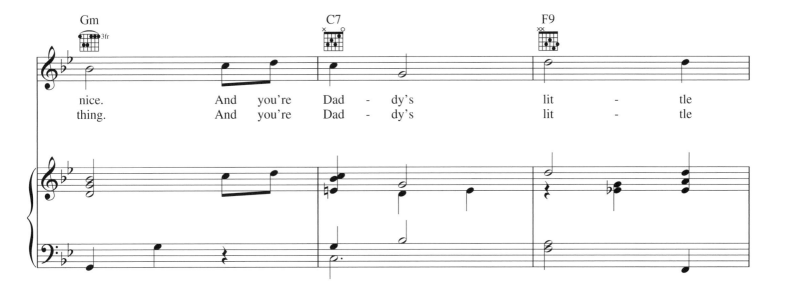

nice. And you're Dad - dy's lit - tle
thing. And you're Dad - dy's lit - tle

girl. _____ You're the girl. _____

I LOVED HER FIRST

Words and Music by WALT ALDRIDGE
and ELLIOT PARK

With a light back-beat

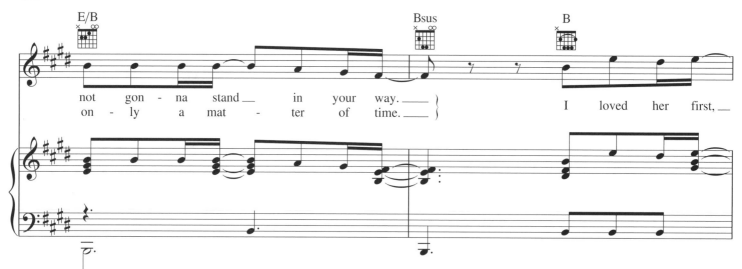

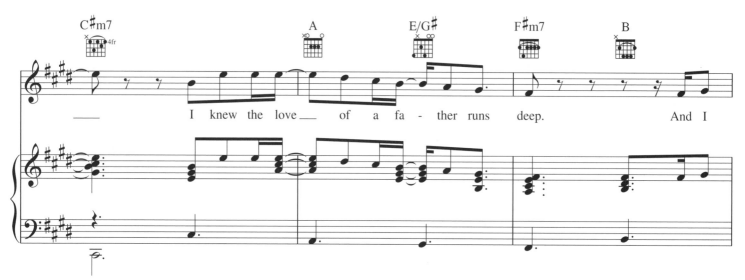

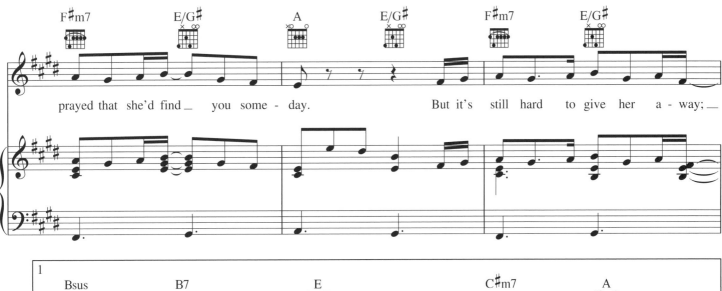

prayed that she'd find __ you some - day. But it's still hard to give her a - way; __

I loved her first. __

I loved her first. __

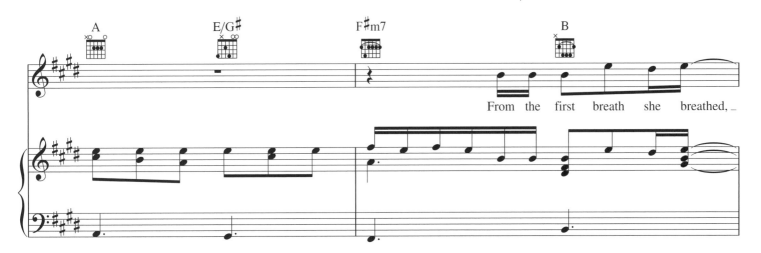

From the first breath she breathed, __

MY GIRL

Words and Music by WILLIAM "SMOKEY" ROBINSON
and RONALD WHITE

I've got sun-shine _____

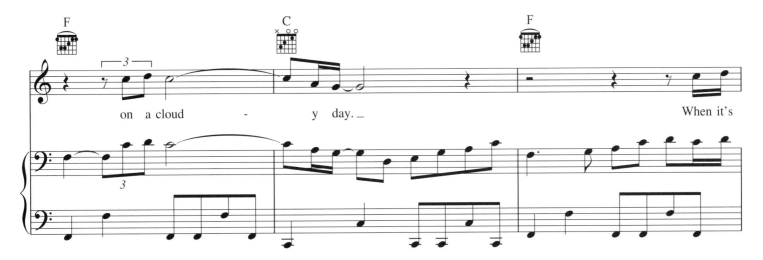

on a cloud - y day. _____   When it's

cold out - side, _____   I've _ got the month of May. _

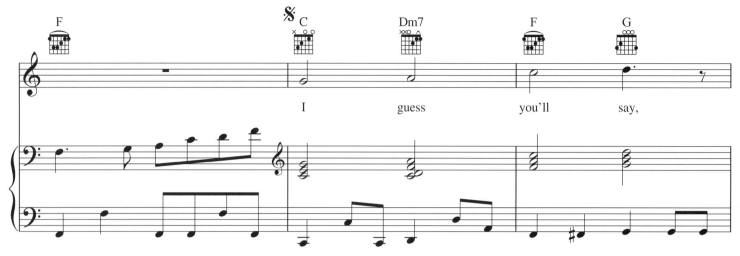

I guess you'll say,

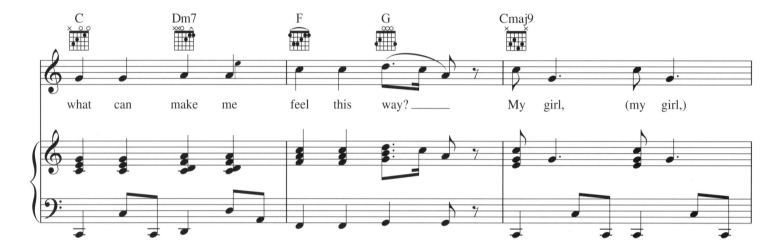

what can make me feel this way? _____ My girl, (my girl,)

(my girl,) talk - in' 'bout _____ my _____ girl. _____

To Coda ⊕

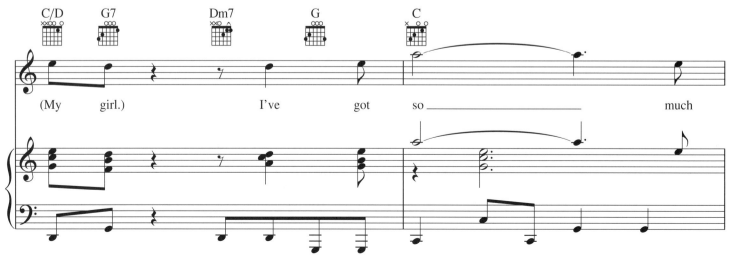

(My girl.) I've got so _____ much

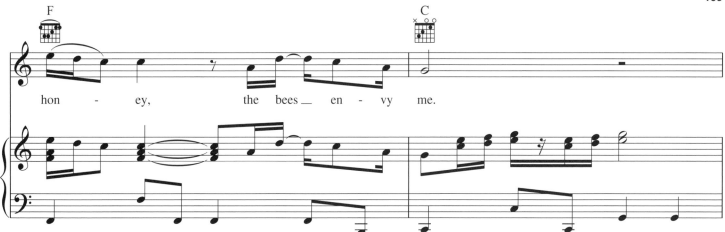

hon - ey, the bees __ en - vy me.

I've got a ____ sweet - er song ____

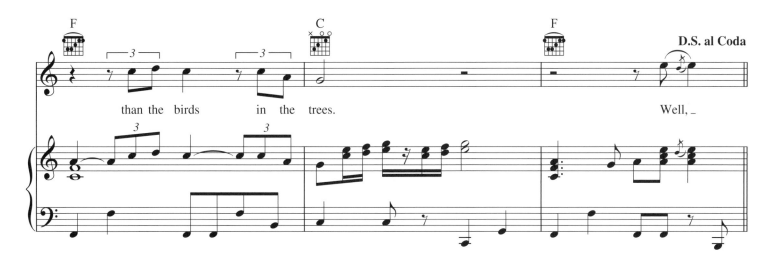

than the birds in the trees.

Well, __

D.S. al Coda

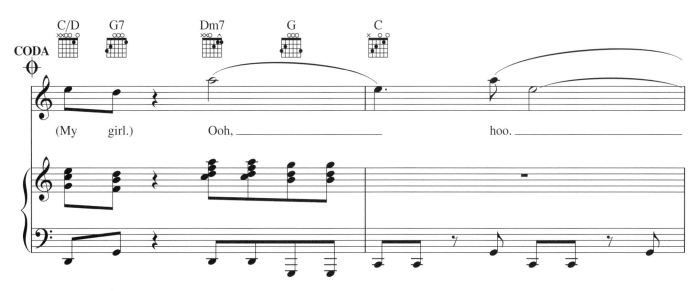

(My girl.) Ooh, ____ hoo. ____

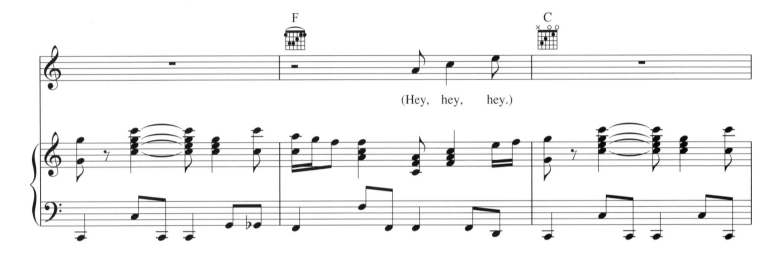

(Hey, hey, hey.)

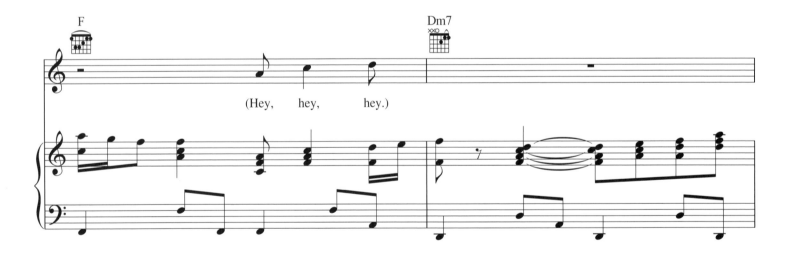

(Hey, hey, hey.)

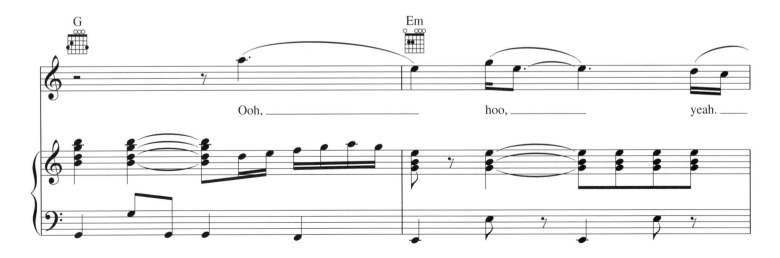

Ooh, _____ hoo, _____ yeah. _____

I don't need no _____ mon - ey, _____

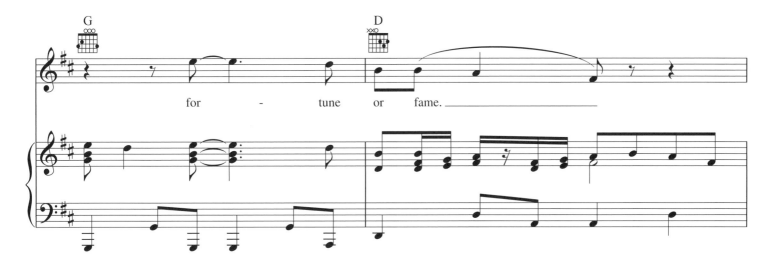

for - tune or fame. _____

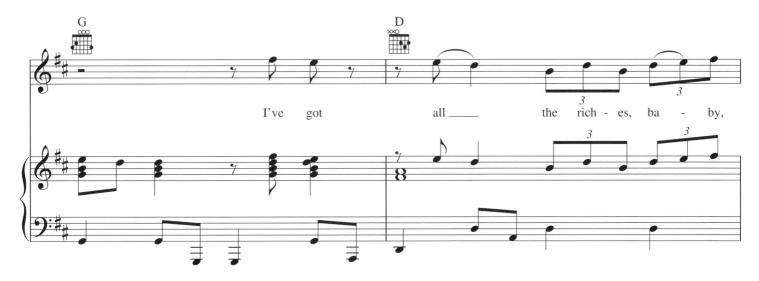

I've got all _____ the rich - es, ba - by,

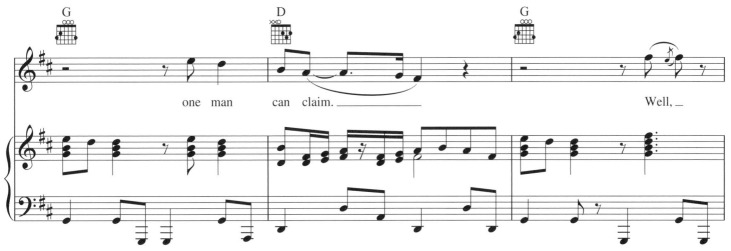

one man can claim. _____ Well, _

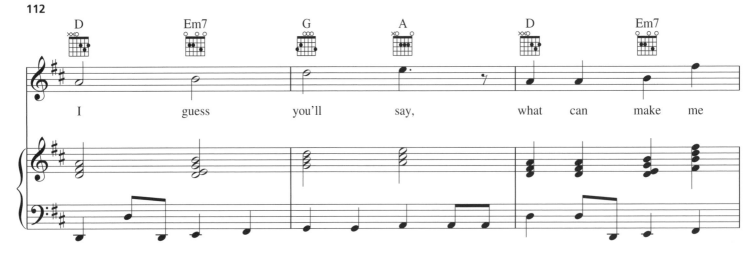

I guess you'll say, what can make me

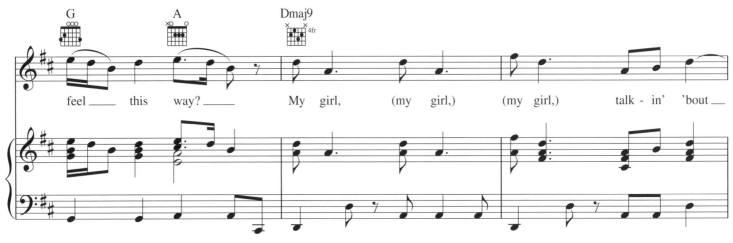

feel ___ this way? ___ My girl, (my girl,) (my girl,) talk - in' 'bout ___

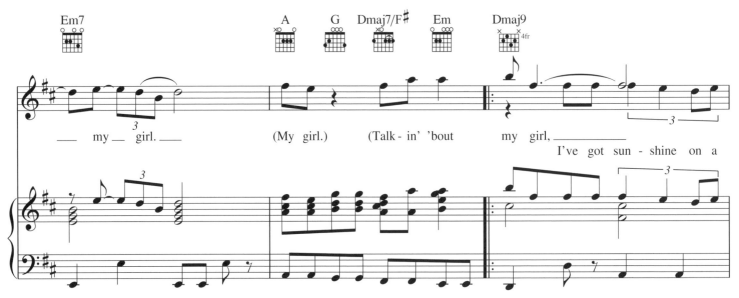

___ my ___ girl. ___ (My girl.) (Talk - in' 'bout my girl, ___ I've got sun - shine on a

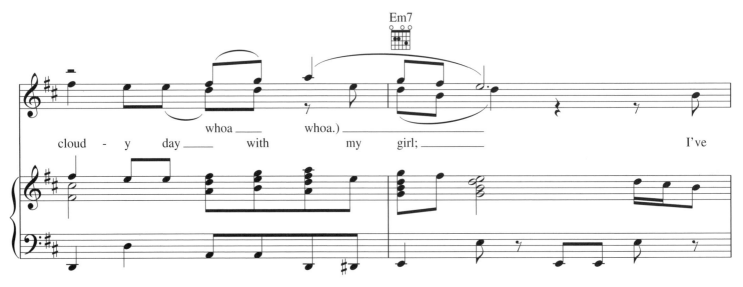

whoa ___ whoa.) ___

cloud - y day ___ with my girl; ___ I've

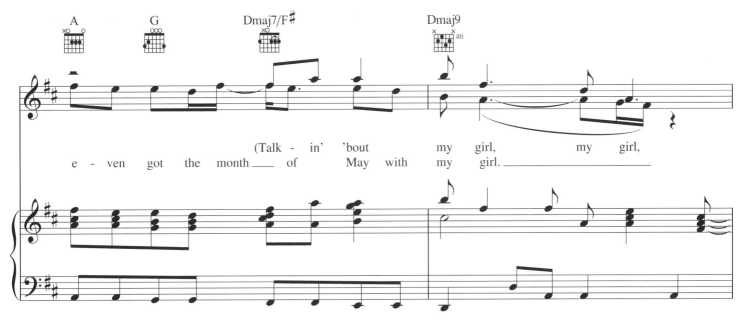

(Talk - in' 'bout   my   girl,   my   girl,

e - ven   got   the   month ___ of   May   with   my   girl. _____

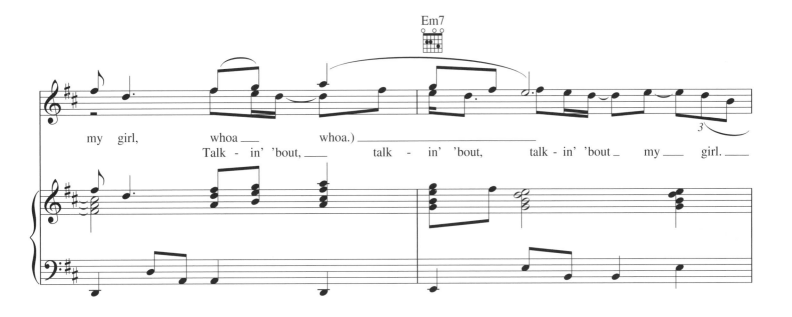

my   girl,   whoa ___   whoa.) _____

Talk - in' 'bout, ___   talk - in' 'bout,   talk - in' 'bout ___ my ___ girl. ___

Repeat and Fade   **Optional Ending**

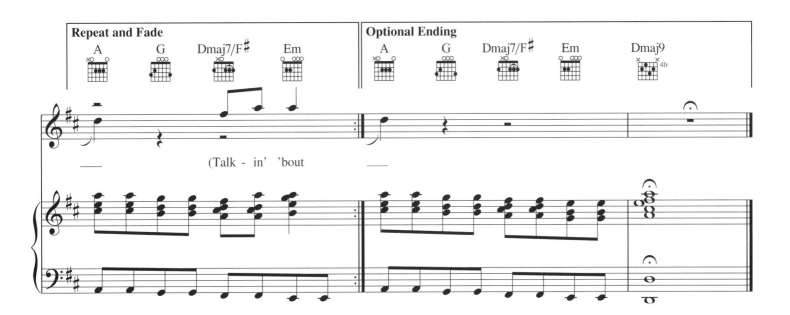

(Talk - in' 'bout ___

MY WISH

Words and Music by STEVE ROBSON
and JEFFREY STEELE

Moderately

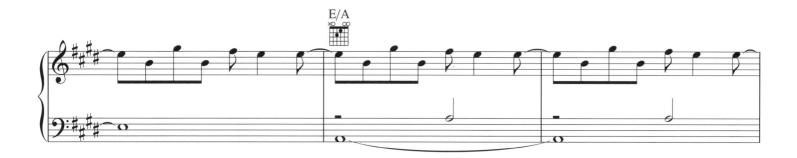

I hope the days come eas-y and the

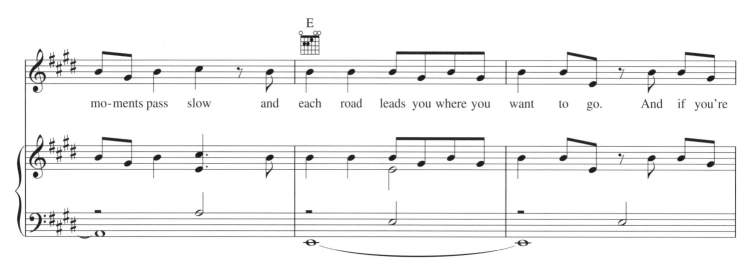

mo-ments pass slow and each road leads you where you want to go. And if you're

faced with the choice and you have to choose, __ I hope you choose the one __ that means the

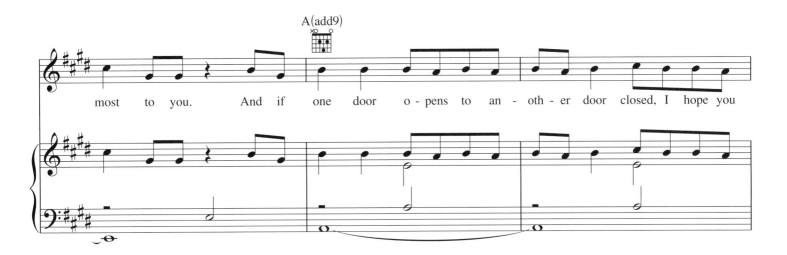

most to you. And if one door o - pens to an - oth - er door closed, I hope you

keep on walk - in' 'til you find the win - dow. If it's cold out - side,

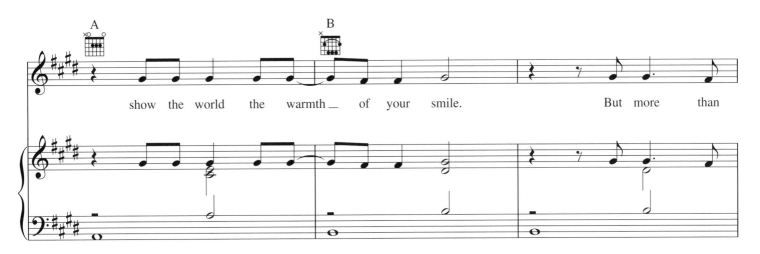

show the world the warmth __ of your smile. But more than

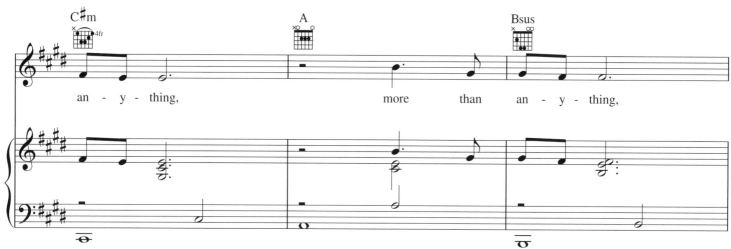

an - y - thing, more than an - y - thing,

my wish for you is that this life ___

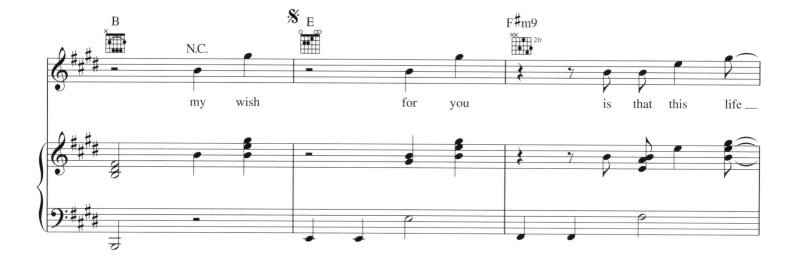

___ be - comes ___ all ___ that you want it to, your dreams stay big, your

wor - ries stay small, you nev - er need to car - ry more than you can hold. And while you're

out there get-tin' where you're get-tin' to, I hope you know some-bod - y loves

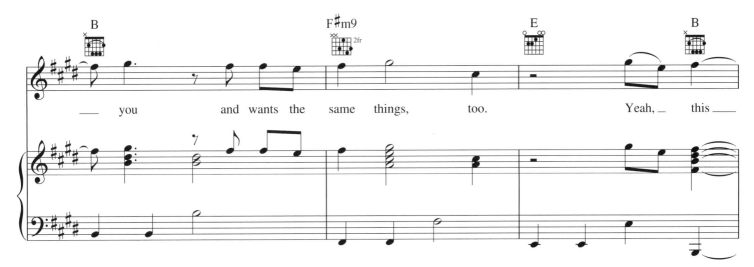

you and wants the same things, too. Yeah, this

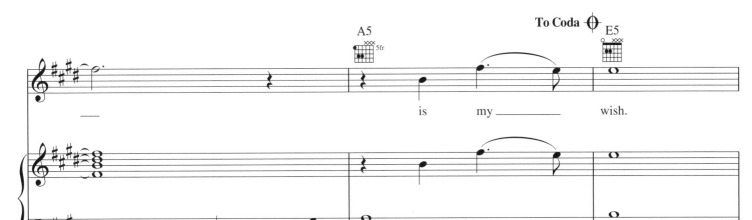

is my wish.

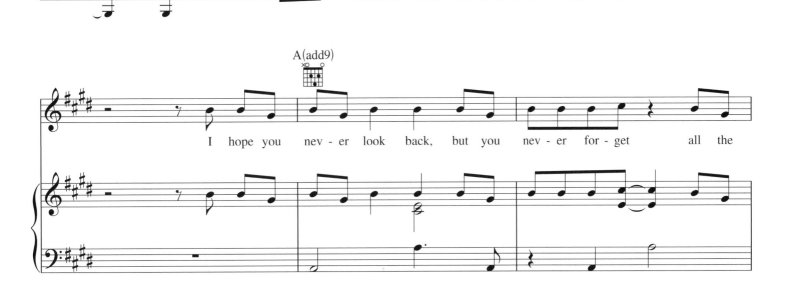

I hope you nev - er look back, but you nev - er for - get all the

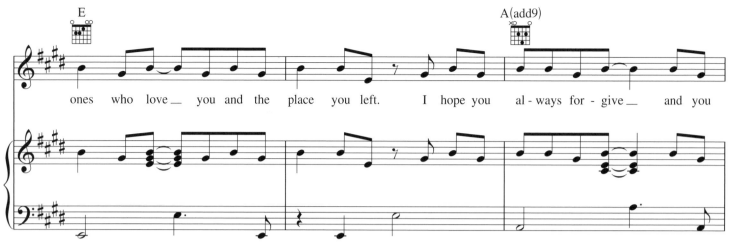

ones who love__ you and the place you left. I hope you al - ways for - give__ and you

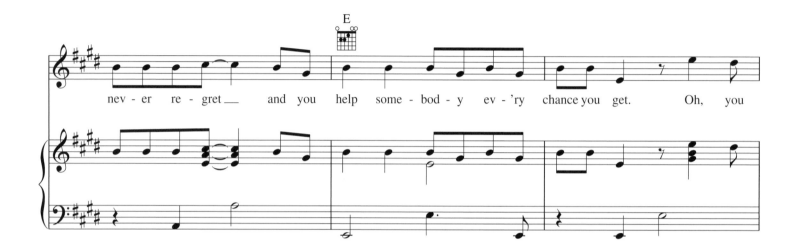

nev - er re - gret__ and you help some - bod - y ev - 'ry chance you get. Oh, you

find__ God's grace in ev - 'ry mis - take and al - ways give more than you take.__

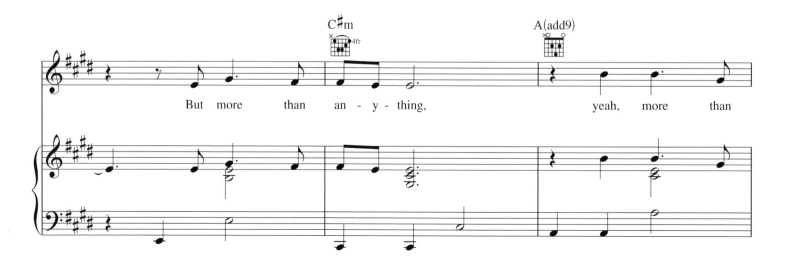

But more than an - y - thing, yeah, more than

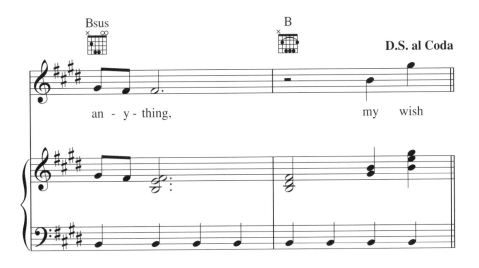
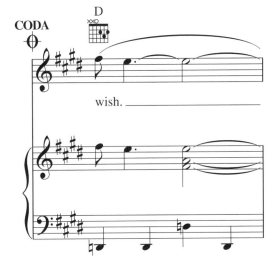
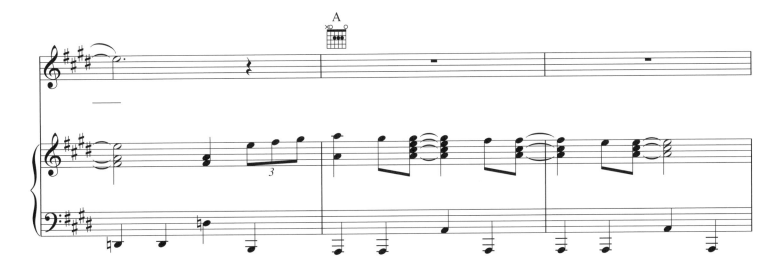
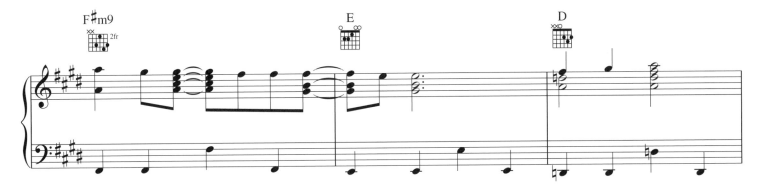
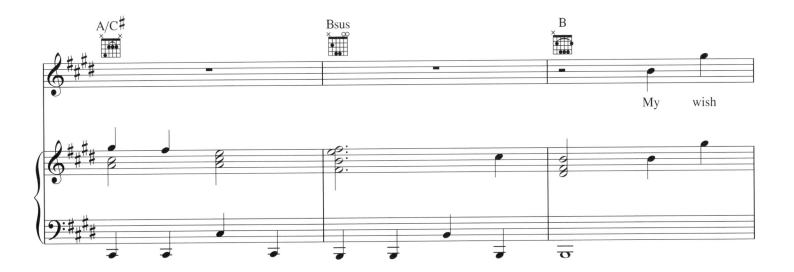

for you   is that this life ___ be-comes all ___

___ that you want it to, your dreams stay big, your wor-ries stay small, you

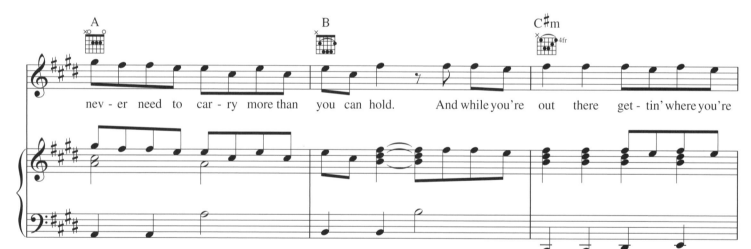

nev-er need to car-ry more than you can hold. And while you're out there get-tin' where you're

get-tin' to, I hope you know some-bod-y loves ___ you and wants the

same things, too. Yeah, __ this _____

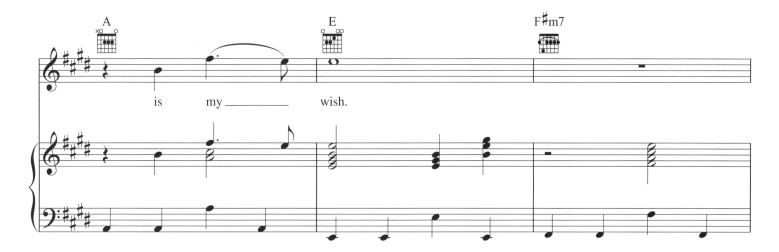

is my _____ wish.

This is my wish.

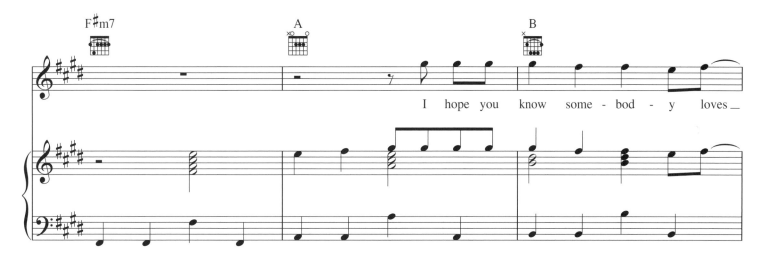

I hope you know some - bod - y loves __

you.

May all

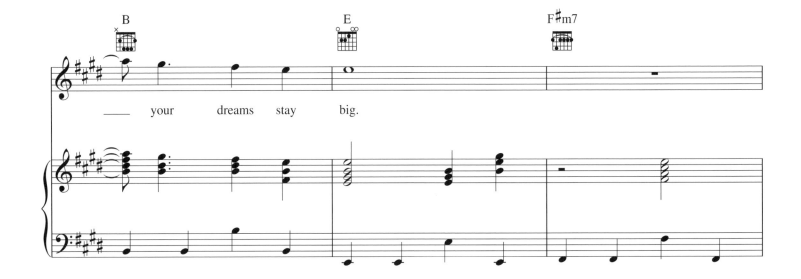

your dreams stay big.

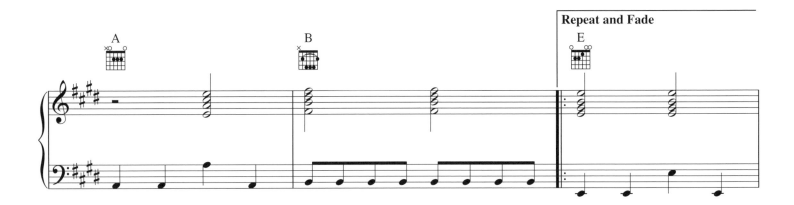

Repeat and Fade

Optional Ending

HAVE I TOLD YOU LATELY

Words and Music by
VAN MORRISON

Slowly, with expression

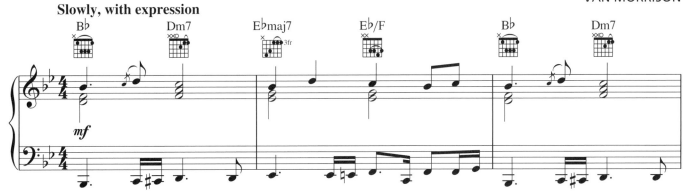

Have I told ___ you late-ly that I love you? Have I

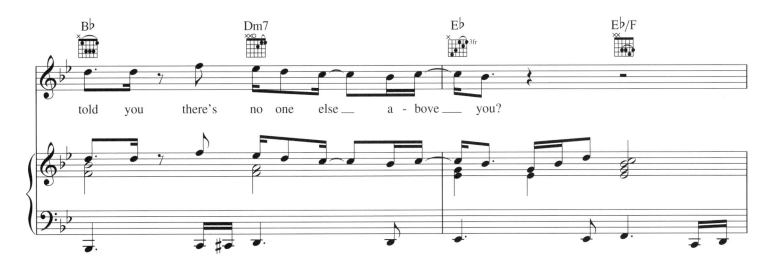

told you there's no one else ___ a-bove ___ you?

Fill my heart ___ with glad - ness, take a-way all ___ my sad - ness,

ease my trou-bles, that's __ what you do.

For the
Instrumental solo

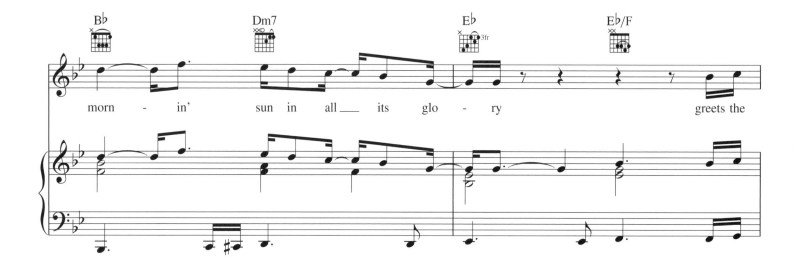

morn - in' sun in all __ its glo - ry

greets the

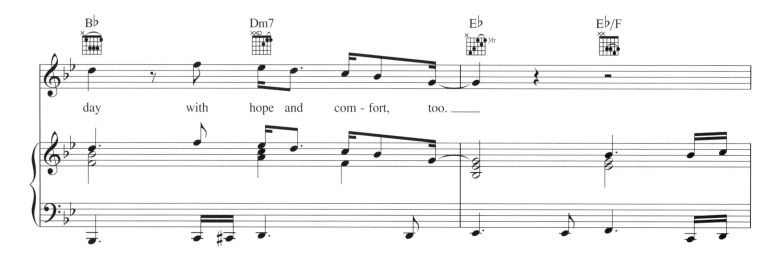

day with hope and com - fort, too. ____

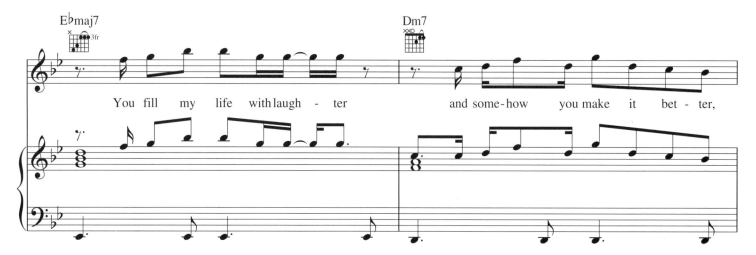

You fill my life with laugh - ter

and some-how you make it bet - ter,

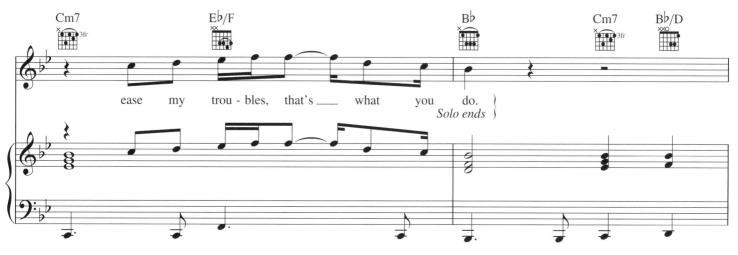

ease my trou-bles, that's ___ what you do.
Solo ends

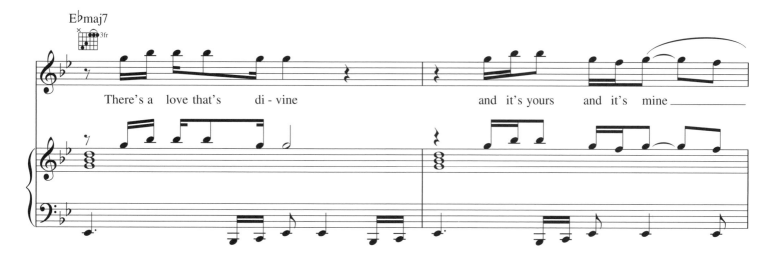

There's a love that's di-vine and it's yours and it's mine ___

___ like the sun. And at the end of the day

we should give thanks and pray ___ to the one, ___ to the one. ___ Have I

to the one. ___ And have I told ___ you late-ly that I

love you? Have I told you there's no one else ___ a-

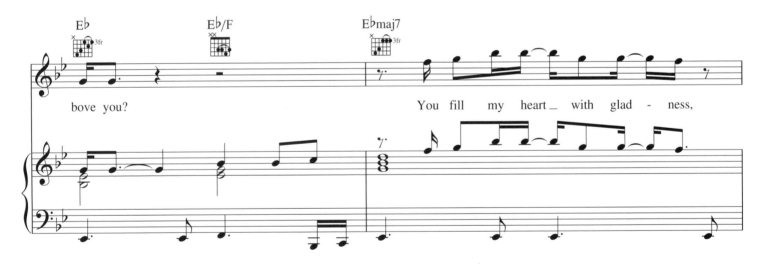

bove you? You fill my heart ___ with glad-ness,

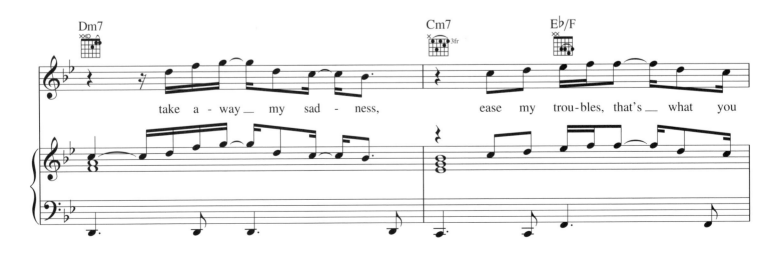

take a-way ___ my sad-ness, ease my trou-bles, that's ___ what you

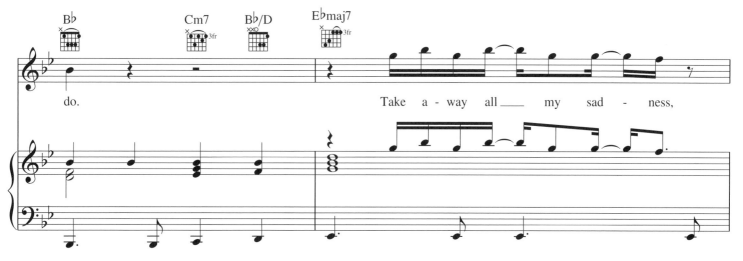

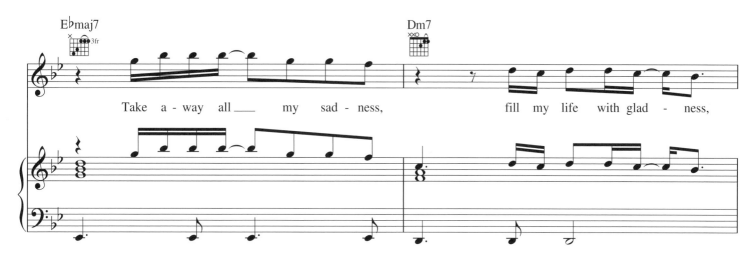

HERO

Words and Music by MARIAH CAREY
and WALTER AFANASIEFF

There's a he - ro if you look in - side __ your heart. You don't
long __ road when you face the world __ a - lone. No one

have to be __ a - fraid of what you are. __ There's an an -
reach - es out __ a hand for you to hold. __ You can find __

- swer if you reach in - to __ your soul __ and the
__ love if you search with - in __ your - self __ and the

sor - row that __ you know __ will melt a - way. _____
emp - ti - ness __ you felt __ will dis - ap - pear. _____

And then a he - ro comes __ a - long __ with the strength to car - ry on __

(D.S. a tempo)

__ and you cast your fears __ a - side __ and you know you can __ sur - vive. __

__ So, when you feel like hope __ is gone, __ look in - side you and __ be strong __

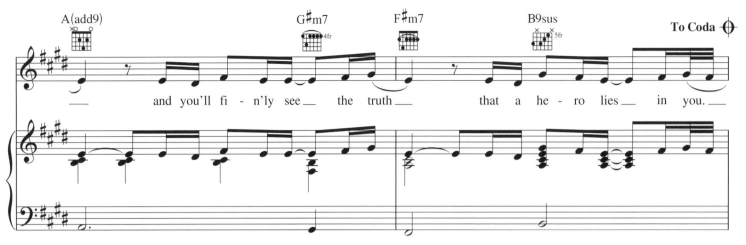

and you'll fi - n'ly see __ the truth __ that a he - ro lies __ in you. __

To Coda

It's a __

Lord knows _____ dreams are hard __ to fol - low,

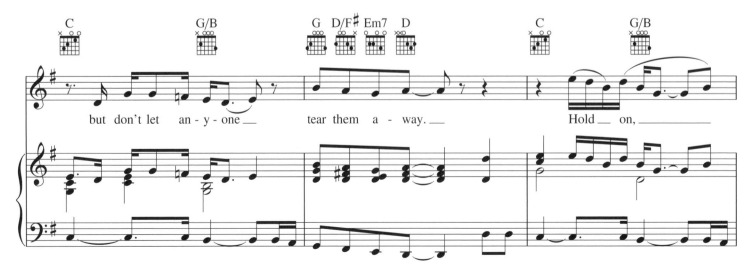

but don't let an - y - one __ tear them a - way. __ Hold __ on, _____

D.S. al Coda

there will be __ to - mor - row. In __ time __ you'll find the way.

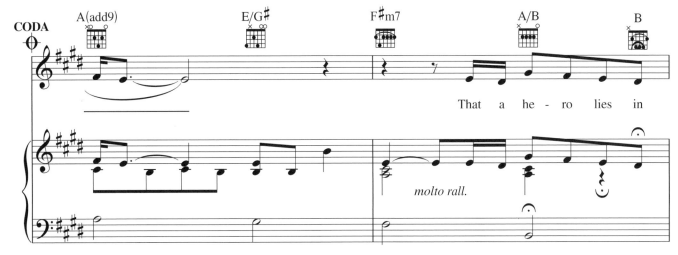

CODA

That a he - ro lies in

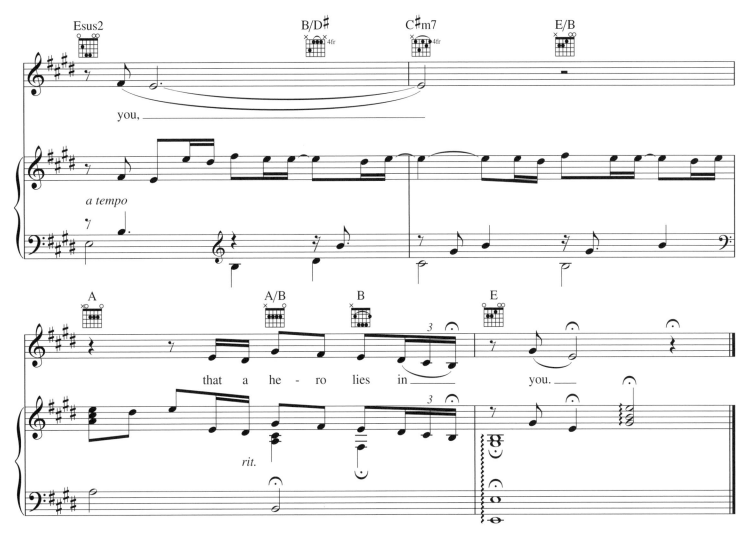

you, __

that a he - ro lies in __ you. __

I HOPE YOU DANCE

Words and Music by TIA SILLERS
and MARK D. SANDERS

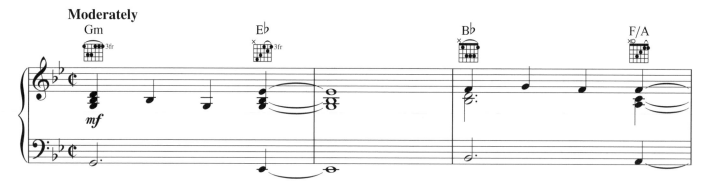

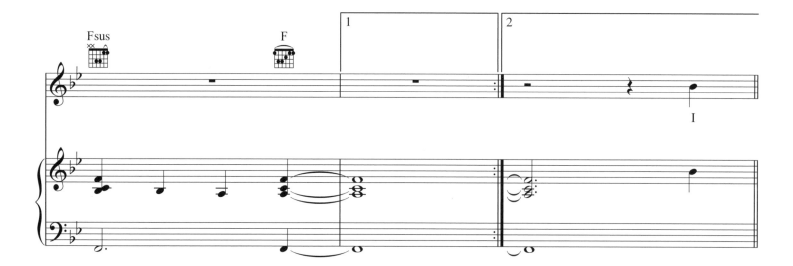

hope you nev- er lose _____ your sense of won- der.
nev- er fear _____ those _____ moun- tains in the dis- tance.

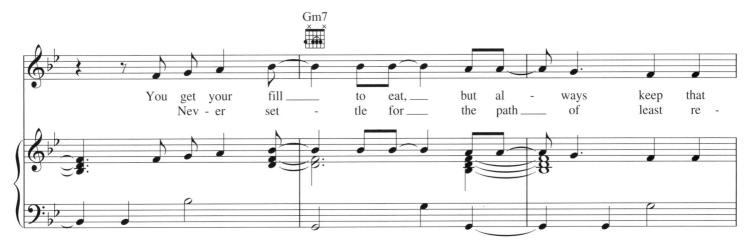

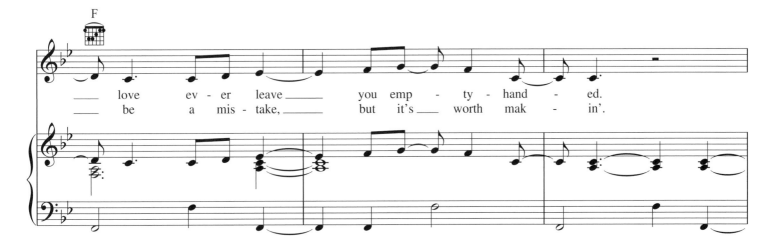

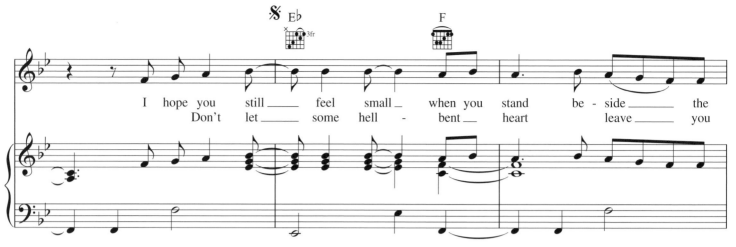

chance.
glance.

And when you get the choice to

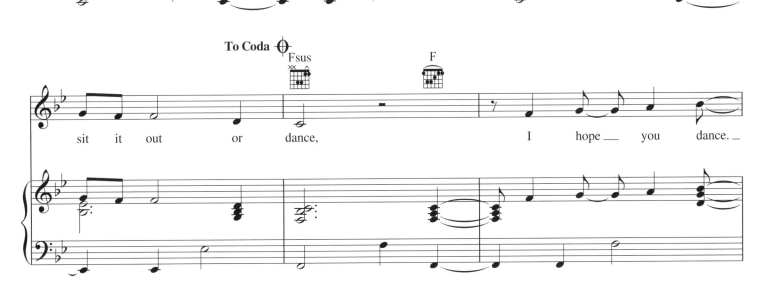

To Coda

sit it out or dance,

I hope you dance.

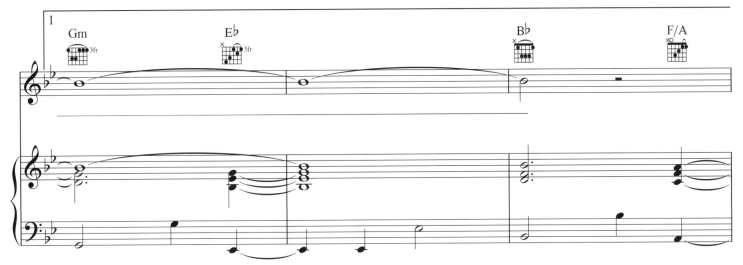

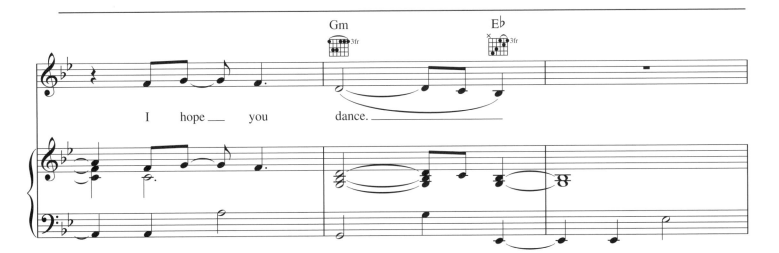

I hope you dance.

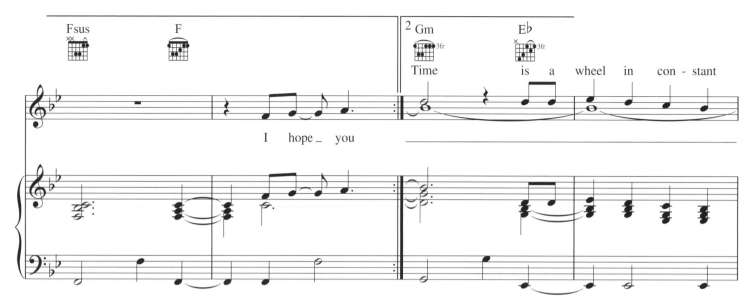

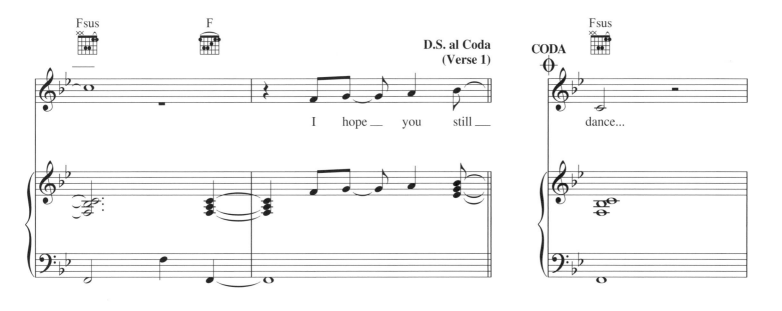

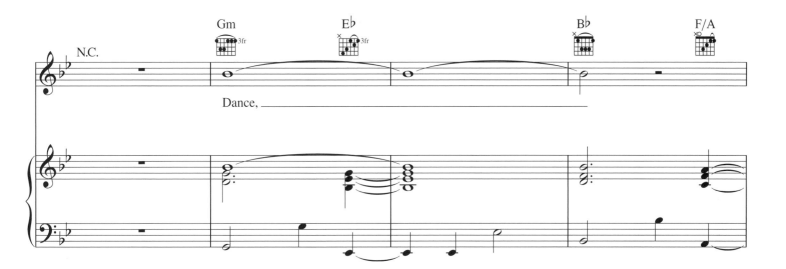

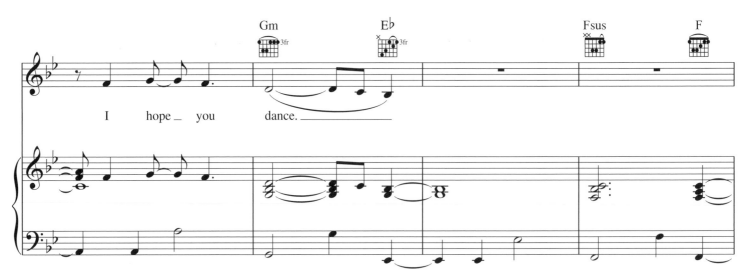

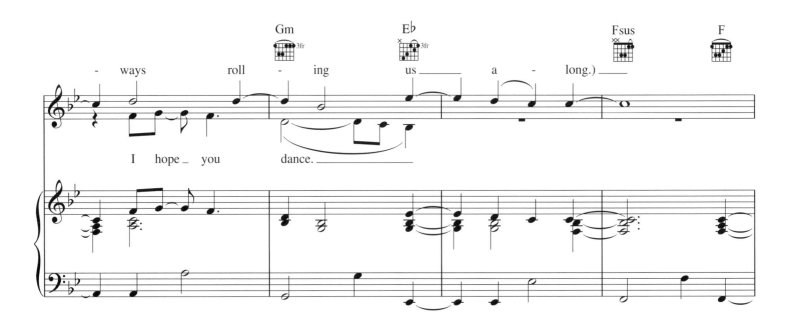

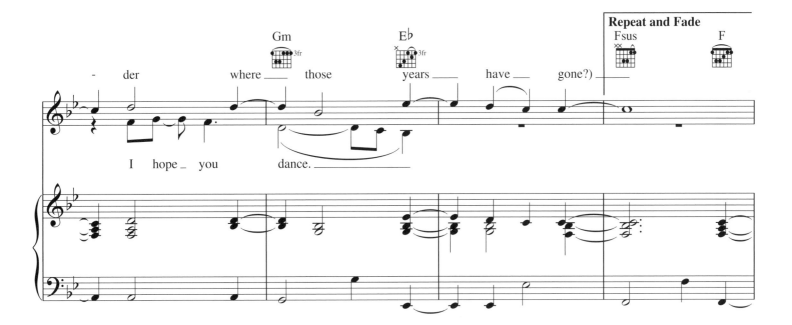

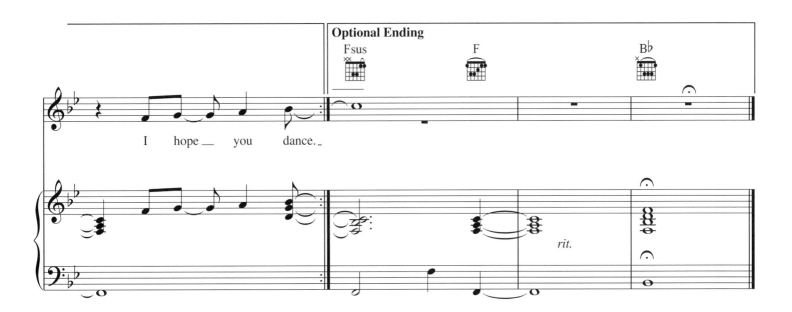

I'LL STAND BY YOU

Words and Music by CHRISSIE HYNDE,
TOM KELLY and BILLY STEINBERG

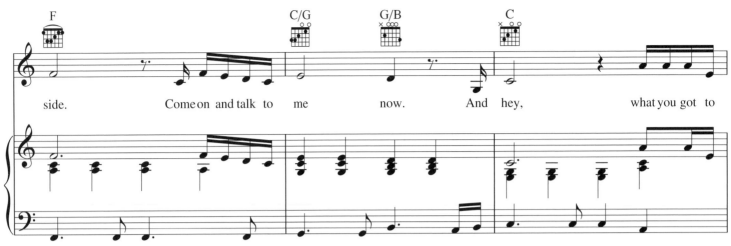

side. Come on and talk to me now. And hey, what you got to

hide? I get an-gry, too. Well, I'm a lot like you.___ When you're

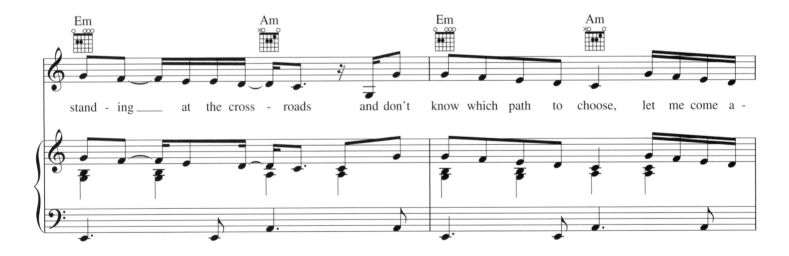

stand - ing___ at the cross - roads and don't know which path to choose, let me come a-

long, 'cause e - ven if you're wrong, I'll stand by

you. I'll stand by you, won't let no-bod-y hurt you. I'll stand by

you. Take me in in-to your dark-est hour, and I'll nev-er de-sert you. I'll stand by

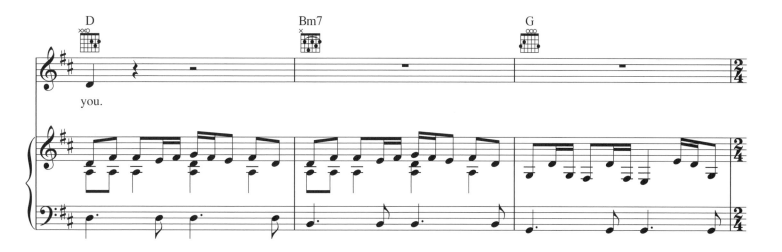

you.

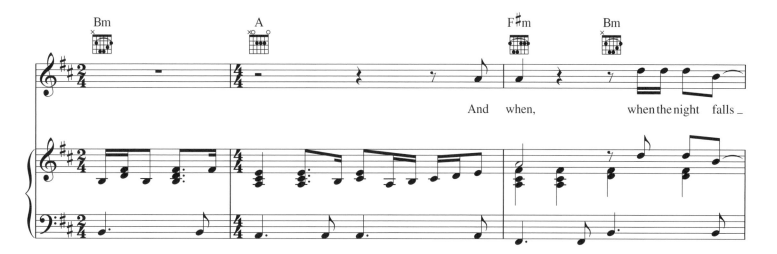

And when, when the night falls

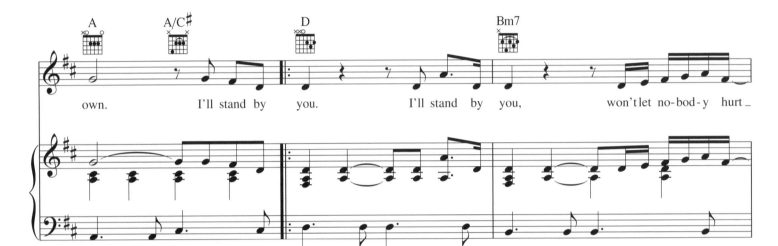

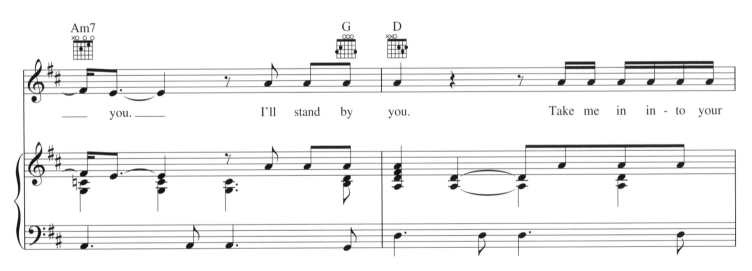

IN MY LIFE

Words and Music by JOHN LENNON
and PAUL McCARTNEY

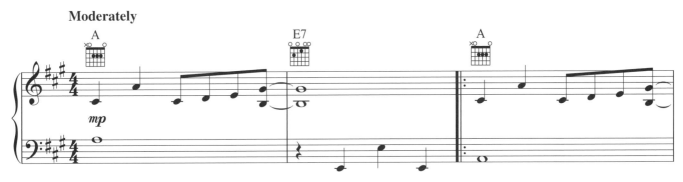

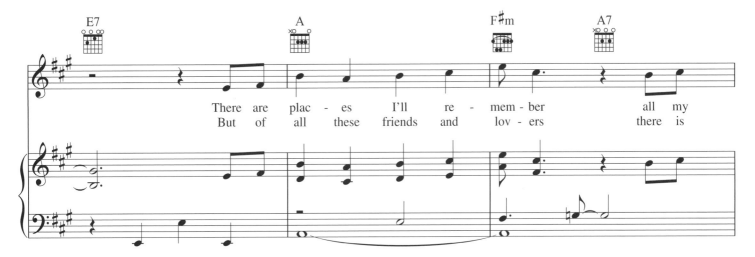

(1.) plac - es __ had __ their __ mo - ments __ with lov - ers and friends __ I
(2.,3.) know __ I'll __ nev - er lose af - fec - tion for peo - ple and things __ that

still can re - call. __ Some are dead __ and __ some __ are __
went __ be - fore, __ I know I'll of - ten stop and think a -

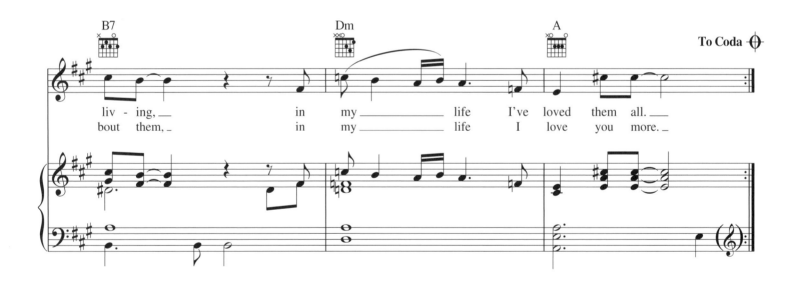

To Coda ⊕

liv - ing, __ in my __ life I've loved them all. __
bout them, __ in my __ life I love you more. __

N.C.

8va -

In 18th century style

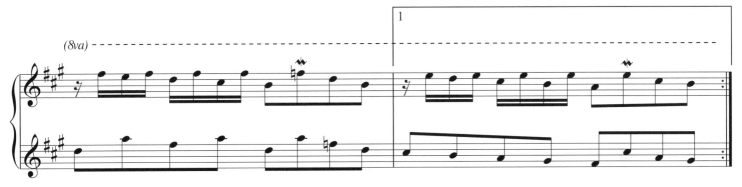

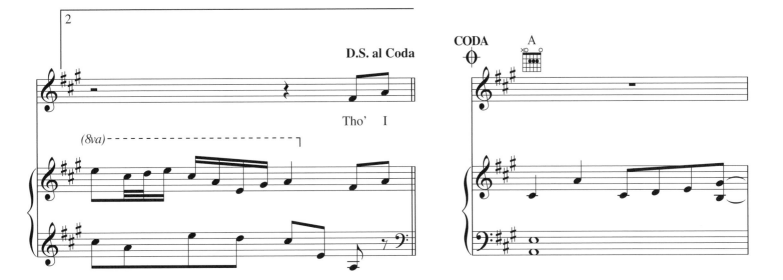

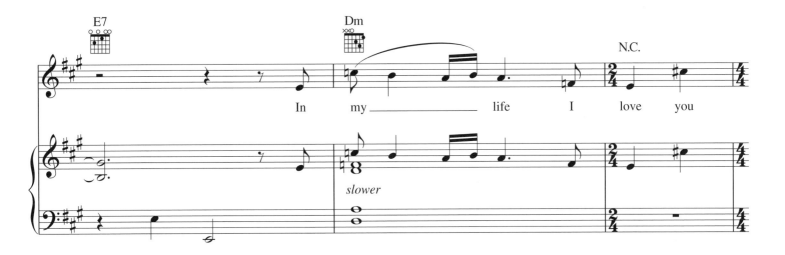

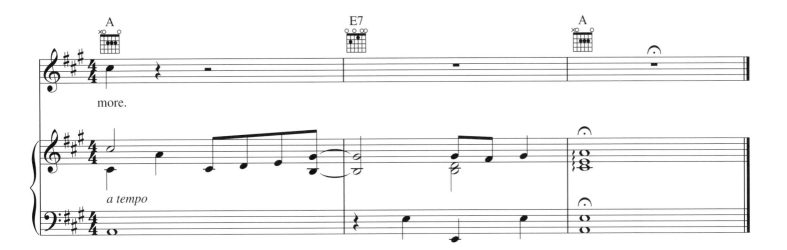

BROWN EYED GIRL

Words and Music by
VAN MORRISON

Moderately

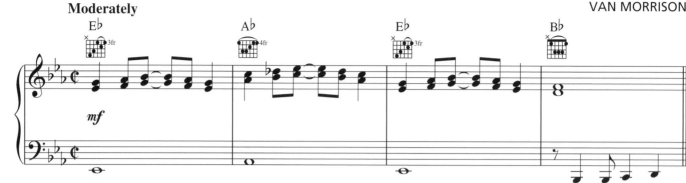

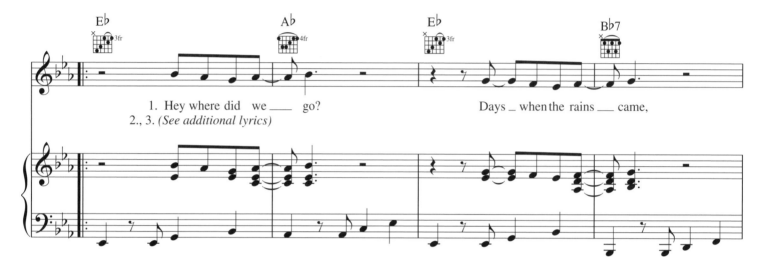

1. Hey where did we ___ go?   Days ___ when the rains ___ came,
2., 3. *(See additional lyrics)*

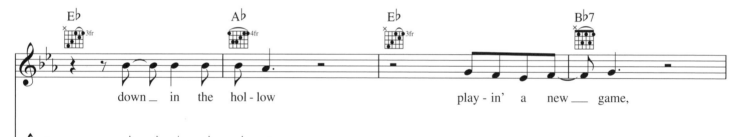

down ___ in the hol-low   play-in' a new ___ game,

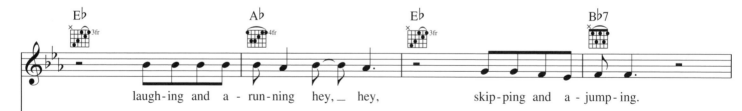

laugh-ing and a-run-ning hey, ___ hey,   skip-ping and a-jump-ing.

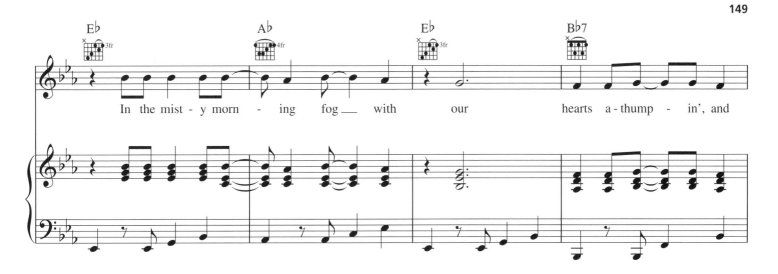

In the mist- y morn - ing fog ___ with our hearts a-thump - in', and

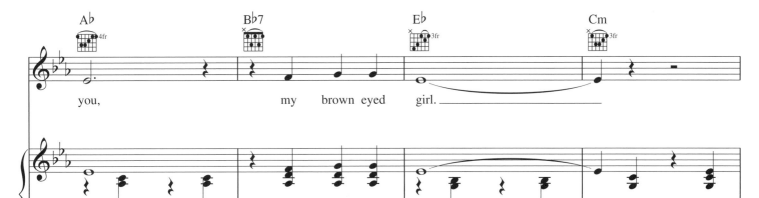

you, my brown eyed girl. _____

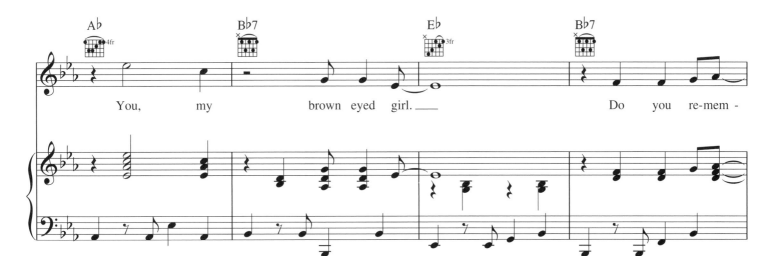

You, my brown eyed girl. ___ Do you re-mem -

Chorus

- ber when we used to sing: ___ sha la ___ la la

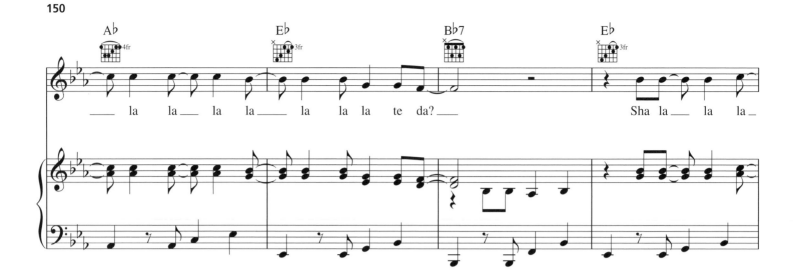

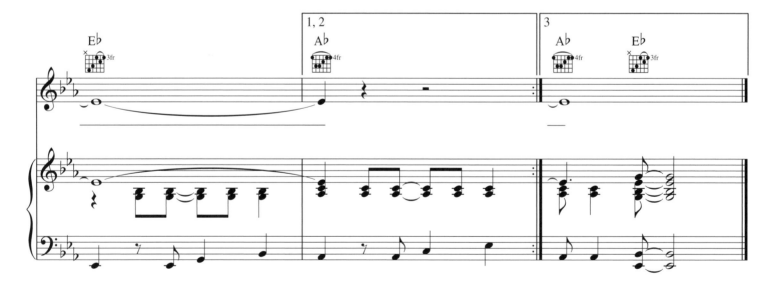

Additional Lyrics

2. Whatever happened to Tuesday and so slow
   Going down the old mine with a transistor radio
   Standing in the sunlight laughing
   Hiding behind a rainbow's wall
   Slipping and a-sliding
   All along the waterfall
   With you, my brown eyed girl
   You, my brown eyed girl.
   Do you remember when we used to sing:
   Chorus

3. So hard to find my way, now that I'm all on my own
   I saw you just the other day, my, how you have grown
   Cast my memory back there, Lord
   Sometime I'm overcome thinking 'bout
   Making love in the green grass
   Behind the stadium
   With you, my brown eyed girl
   With you, my brown eyed girl.
   Do you remember when we used to sing:
   Chorus

Dancing Queen

Words and Music by BENNY ANDERSSON,
BJÖRN ULVAEUS and STIG ANDERSON

Strong Rock

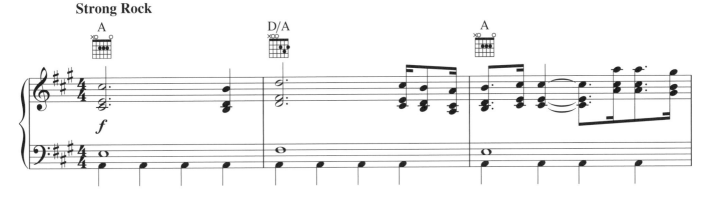

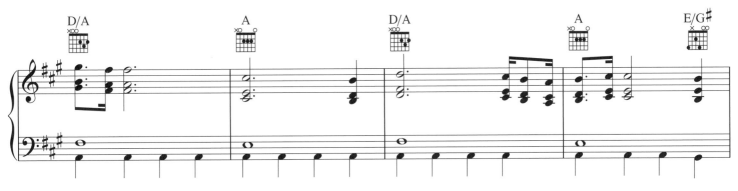

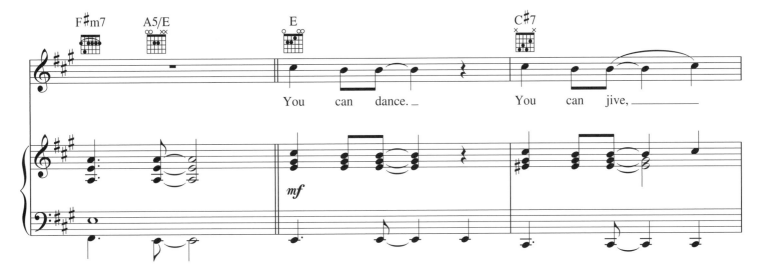

You can dance. You can jive, having the time of your life. Oh, see that girl.

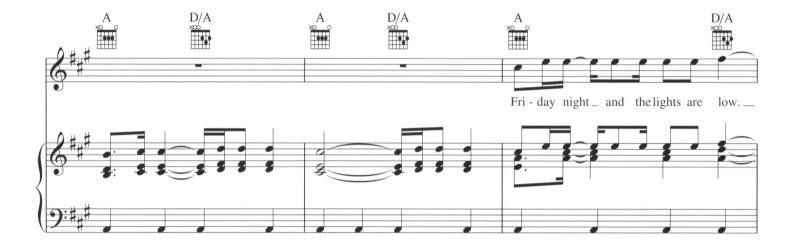

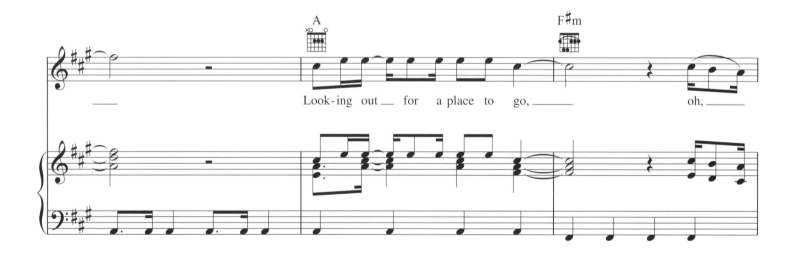

young and __ sweet, __ on - ly sev - en - teen. __

Danc - ing __ queen, __ feel the __ beat __ from the tam - bou - rine. __

__ You can dance. __ You can jive, __

hav - ing __ the time of __ your life. __ Oh, __ see that __ girl. __

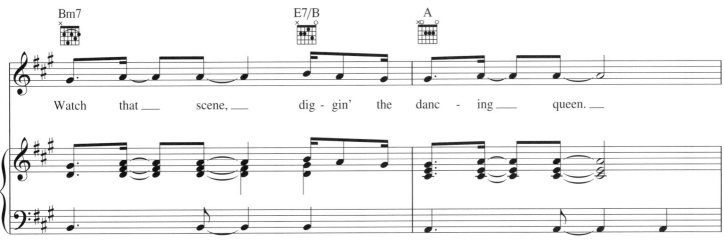

Watch that ___ scene, ___ dig - gin' the danc - ing ___ queen. ___

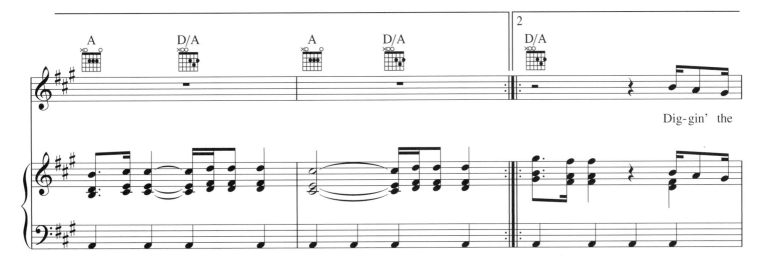

Dig - gin' the

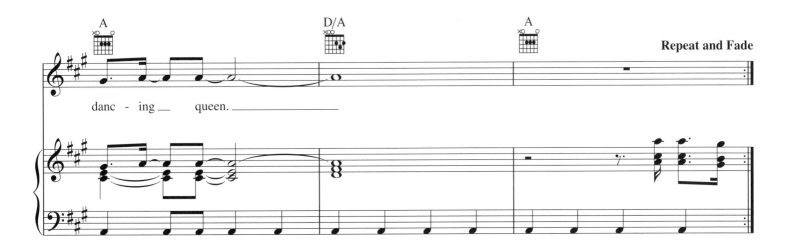

danc - ing ___ queen. ___

Repeat and Fade

FIREWORK

Words and Music by MIKKEL ERIKSEN,
TOR ERIK HERMANSEN, ESTHER DEAN,
KATY PERRY and SANDY WILHELM

Dance Pop

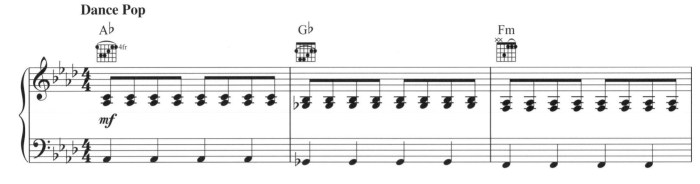

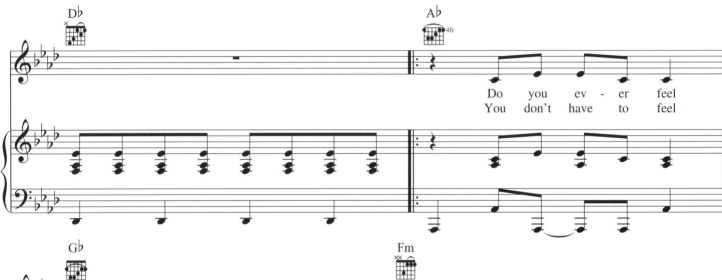

Do you ev - er feel
You don't have to feel

like a plas - tic bag, drift - ing through the wind,
like a wast - ed space. You're o - rig - i - nal,

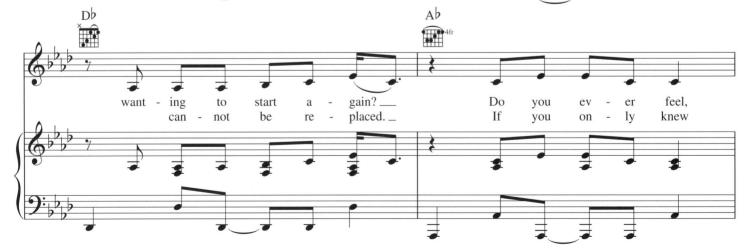

want - ing to start a - gain? Do you ev - er feel,
can - not be re - placed. If you on - ly knew

feel so pa – per thin, like a house of cards,
what the fu – ture holds, af – ter a hur – ri – cane

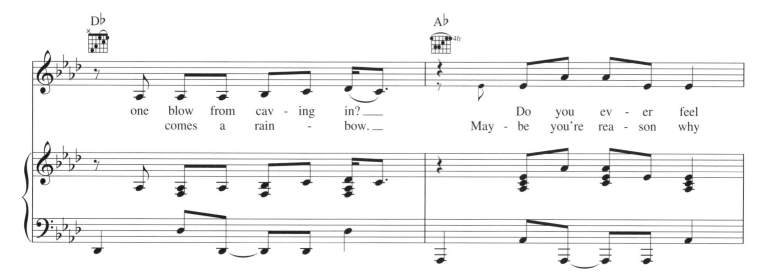

one blow from cav – ing in? ___ Do you ev – er feel
comes a rain – bow. ___ May – be you're rea – son why

al – read – y bur – ied deep, six feet un – der screams, but
all the doors are closed. So you could o – pen one that

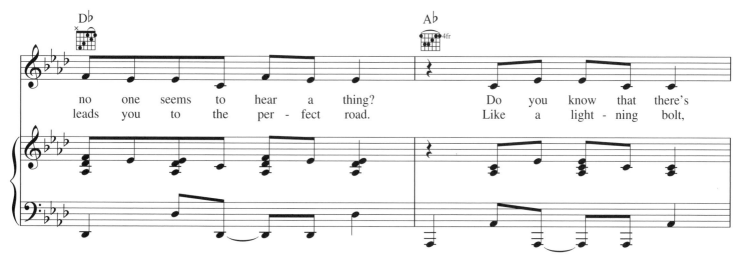

no one seems to hear a thing? Do you know that there's
leads you to the per – fect road. Like a light – ning bolt,

still a chance for you?
your heart will glow;

'Cause there's a spark in you.
and when it's time, we know.

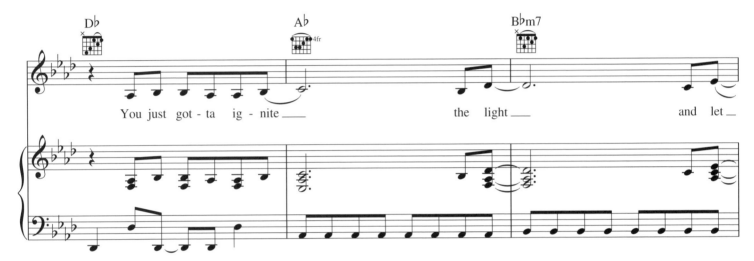

You just got-ta ig - nite ___ the light ___ and let ___

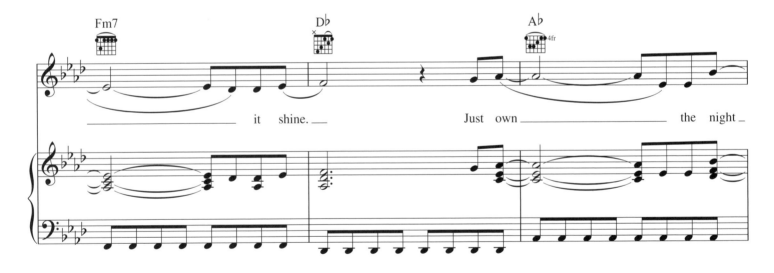

___ it shine. ___ Just own ___ the night ___

___ like the Fourth ___ of ___ Ju - ly. ___ 'Cause, ba - by, you're a

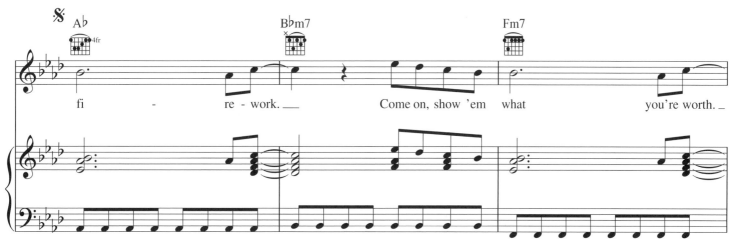

fi - re - work. __ Come on, show 'em what you're worth. __

__ Make 'em go, __ "Ah, ah, __ ah," as you shoot a-cross the

sky - y - y. Ba-by, you're a fi - re-work. __

__ Come on, let your col - ors burst. __ Make 'em go, __

To Coda

"Ah, ah, ___ ah."   You're gon-na leave 'em all in awe, awe, ___ awe. ___

Boom, boom, ___ boom,   e-ven bright-er than the

moon, moon, ___ moon.   It's al-ways been in-side of you, ___ you, ___ you,

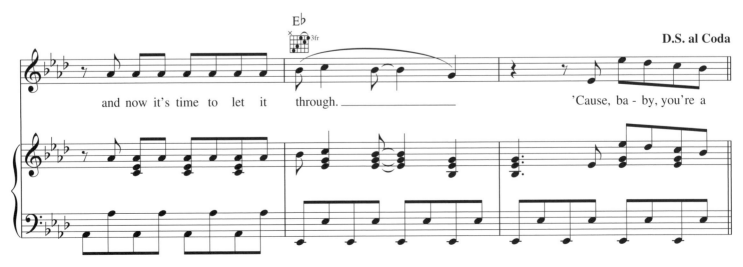

and now it's time to let it   through. ___   'Cause, ba-by, you're a

D.S. al Coda

I GOTTA FEELING

Words and Music by WILL ADAMS,
ALLAN PINEDA, JAIME GOMEZ,
STACY FERGUSON, DAVID GUETTA
and FREDERIC RIESTERER

Moderately fast

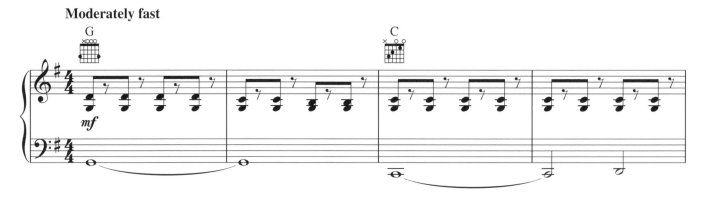

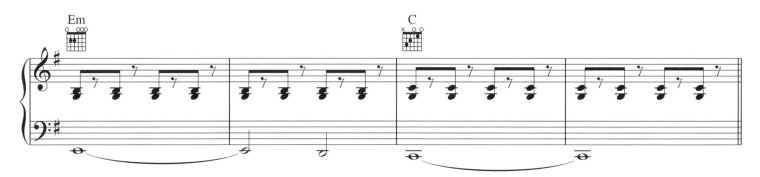

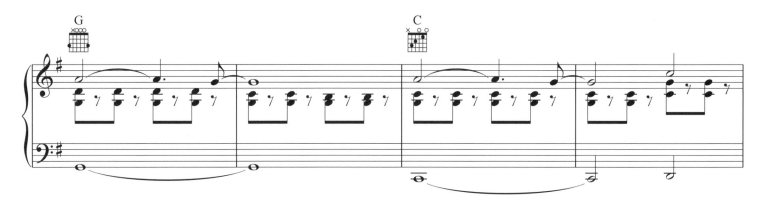

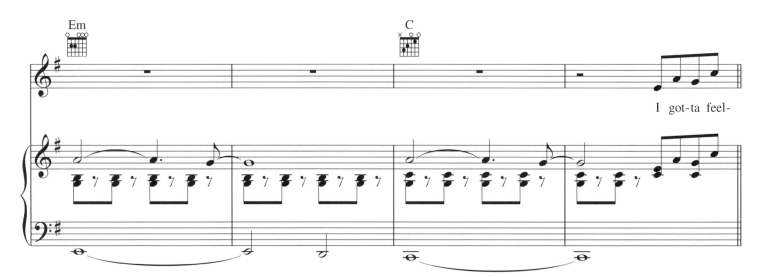

I got-ta feel-

ing

that to - night's _ gon - na be _ a good _

_ night, _ that to - night's _ gon - na be _ a good _ night, _ that to - night's _

_ gon - na be _ a good, _ good night. _ A feel - ing

(Woo -

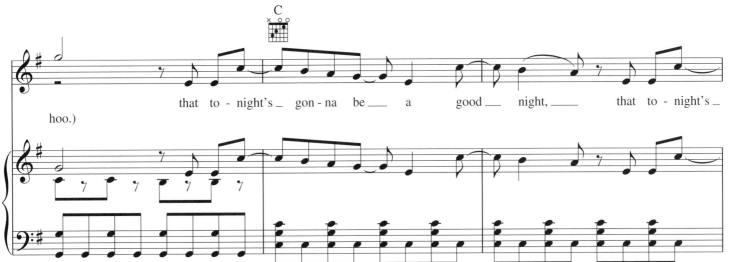

that to - night's _ gon - na be _ a good _ night, _ that to - night's _

hoo.)

Let's burn the roof,
Woo.) _____
and then we'll do it a - gain. _____ Let's do it, let's

do it, let's do it, let's do it, ___ and do it, and do it. Let's live it up, and

do it, and do it, and do it, do it, do it. Let's do it. Let's do it. Let's

do it, do it, do it, do it. Here we come, here we go. We got - ta rock.

Par - ty ev -'ry day. P - P - P - Par - ty ev -'ry day. And I'm feel - ing (Woo

hoo.) that to - night's _ gon - na be _ a good _ night, _ that to - night's _

_ gon - na be _ a good _ night, _ that to - night's _ gon - na be _ a good, _

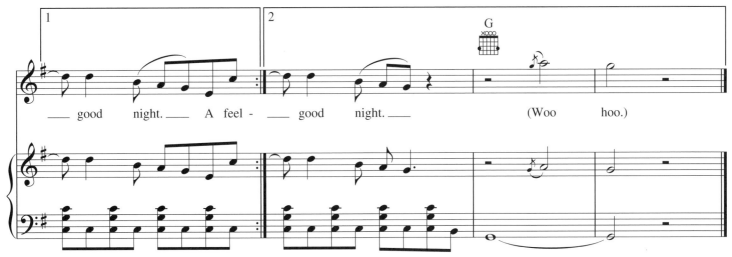

1
_ good night. _ A feel - _ good night. _

2
(Woo hoo.)

SWEET CAROLINE

Words and Music by
NEIL DIAMOND

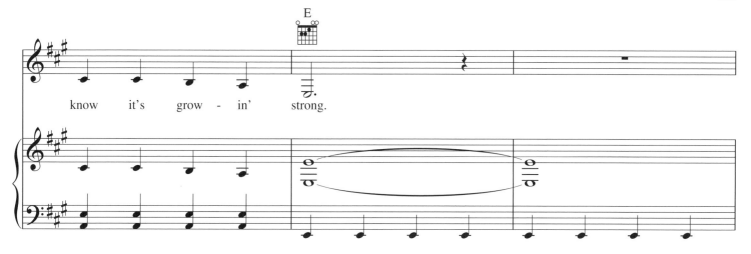

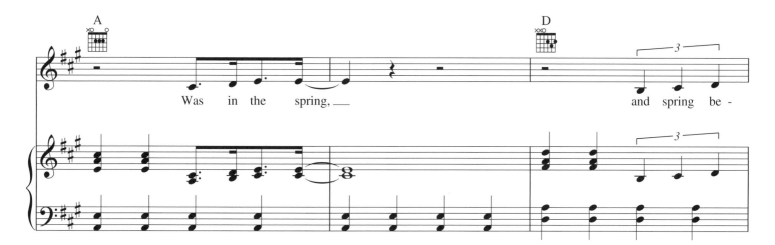

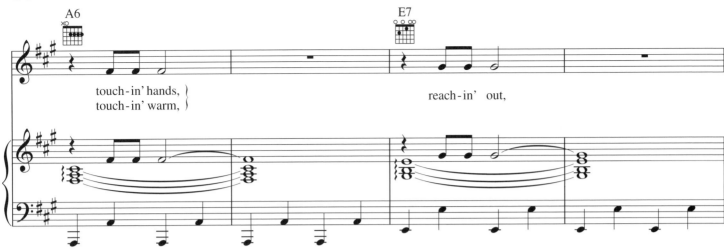

touch-in' hands, }
touch-in' warm, }

reach-in' out,

touch-in' me

touch-in' you. _____

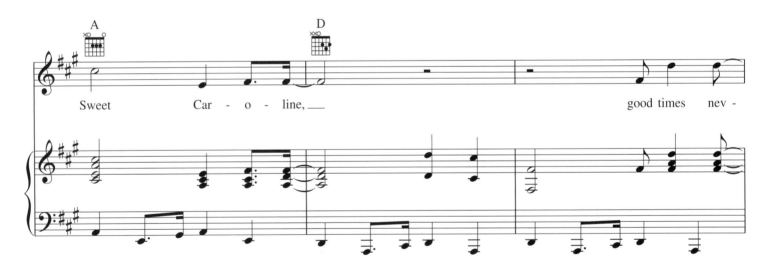

Sweet   Car - o - line, ___

good times nev -

- er   seemed so good.

I've been in- clined __ to be - lieve _

__ they nev - er would.
{But now I
{Oh, now no, I no.

look at the night, _

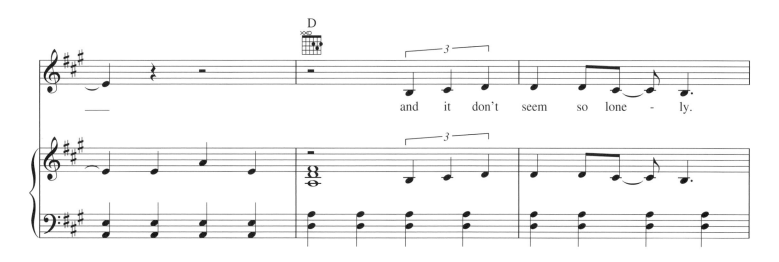

__

and it don't seem so lone - ly.

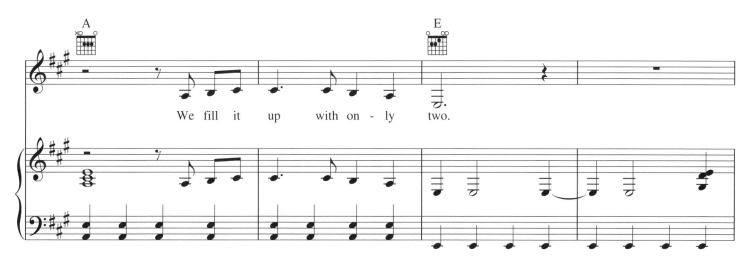

We fill it up with on - ly two.

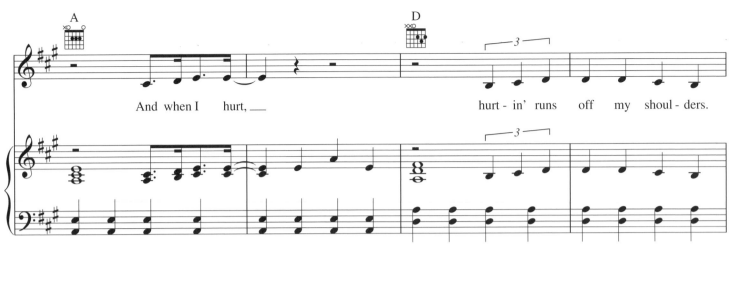

And when I hurt, ___ hurt - in' runs off my shoul - ders.

How can I hurt ___ when hold - in' you? ___

D.S. al Coda

CODA

N.C.

TEQUILA

By CHUCK RIO

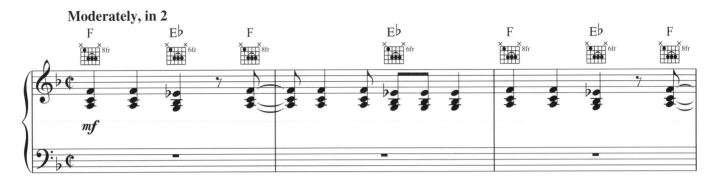

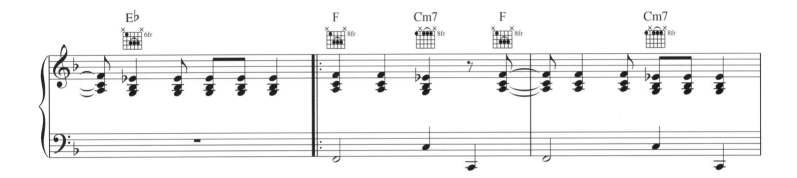

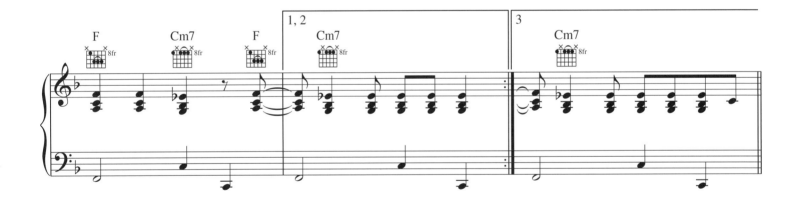

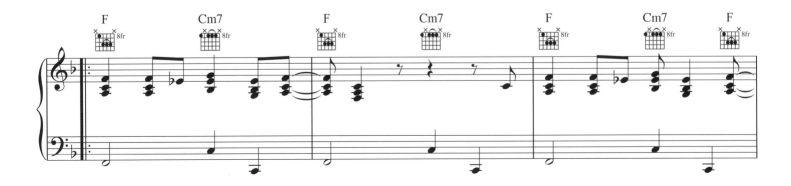

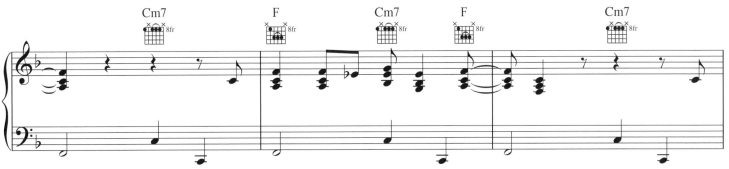

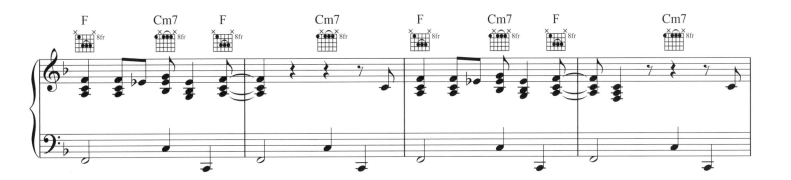

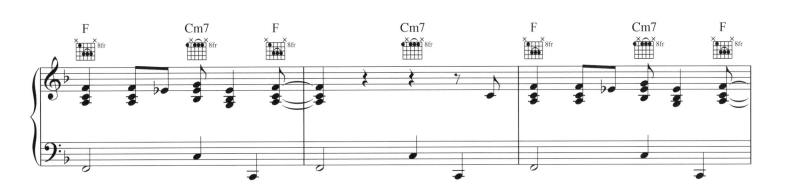

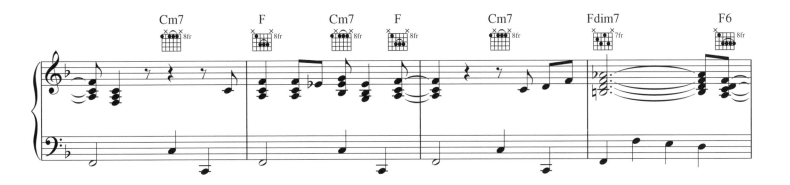

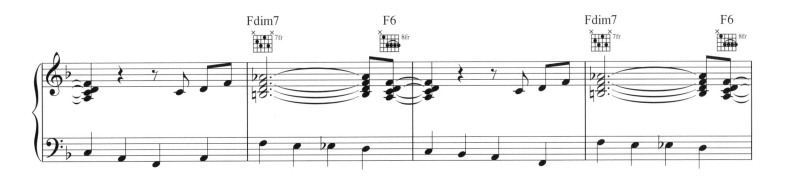

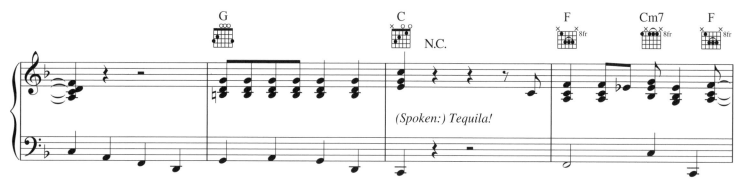

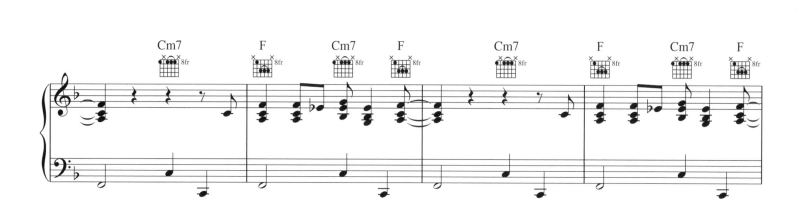

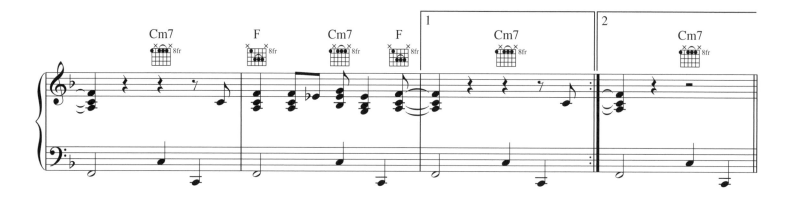

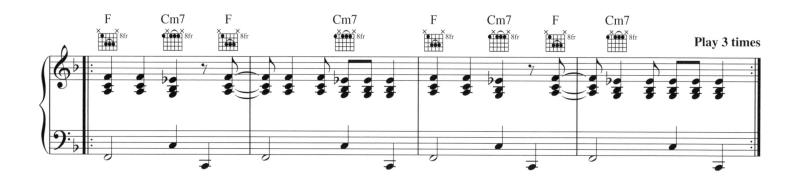

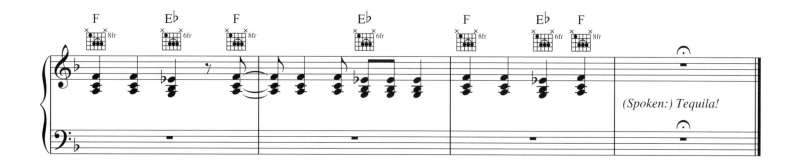

THE EDGE OF GLORY

Words and Music by STEFANI GERMANOTTA,
PAUL BLAIR and FERNANDO GARIBAY

There ain't no rea- son you and me should be a- lone to- night,___
An- oth- er shot___ be- fore we kiss the oth- er side to- night,___

___ yeah, ba- by, to- night,_____ yeah, ba- by.
___ yeah, ba- by, to- night,_____ yeah, ba- by.

But I've got a rea- son that you_____ should take me home to- night._
I'm on the edge___ of some- thing fi- nal we call life to- night,_

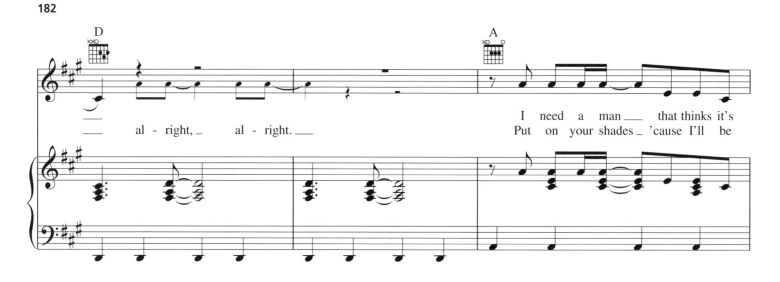

al - right, _ al - right. _
I need a man _ that thinks it's
Put on your shades _ 'cause I'll be

right when it's so wrong, to - night, _____ yeah, ba - by, to - night, _
danc - ing in the flames to - night, _____ yeah, ba - by, to - night, _

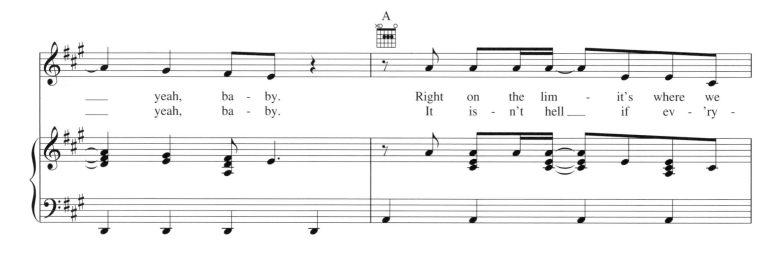

_ yeah, ba - by. Right on the lim - it's where we
_ yeah, ba - by. It is - n't hell _ if ev - 'ry -

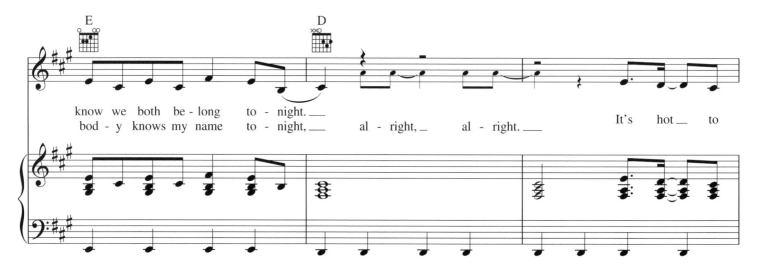

know we both be - long to - night. _
bod - y knows my name to - night, _ al - right, _ al - right. _
It's hot _ to

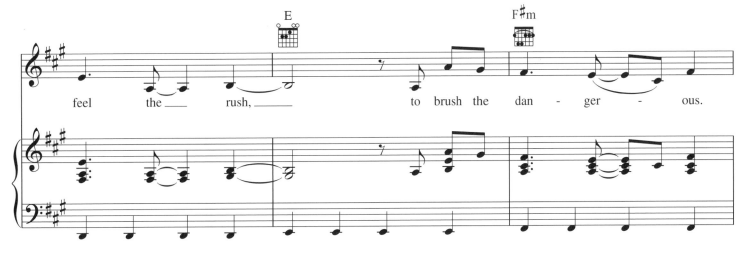

feel the ___ rush, ___ to brush the dan - ger - ous.

I'm gon - na run right to, ___ to the edge ___ with you, ___ where we can

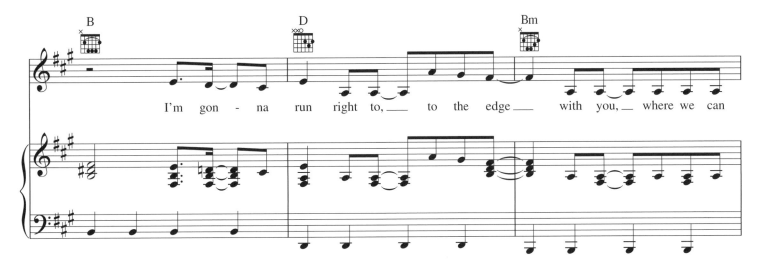

both fall ___ far ___ in love. ___ I'm on the edge ___ of glo -

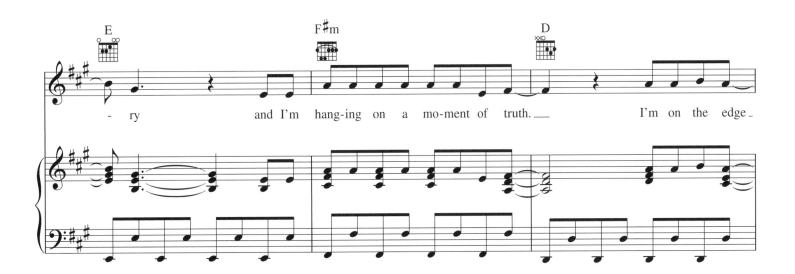

- ry and I'm hang-ing on a mo-ment of truth. ___ I'm on the edge ___

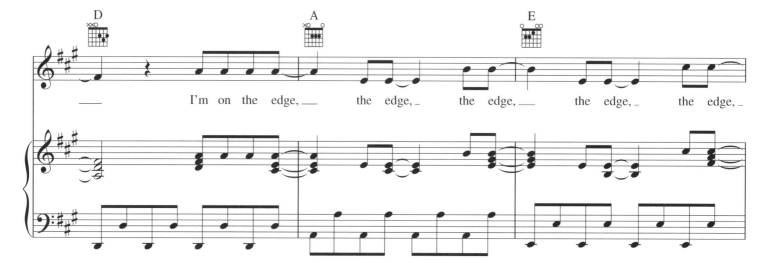

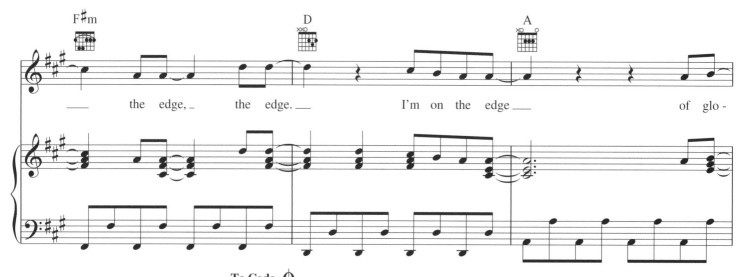

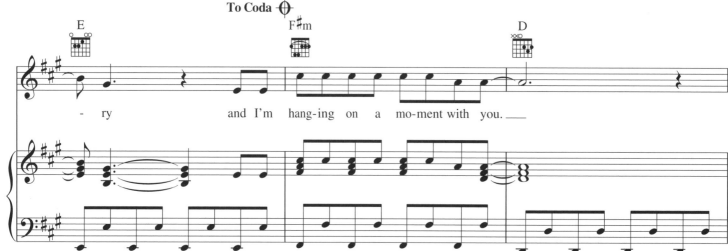

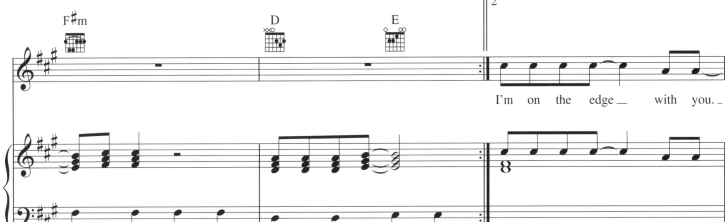

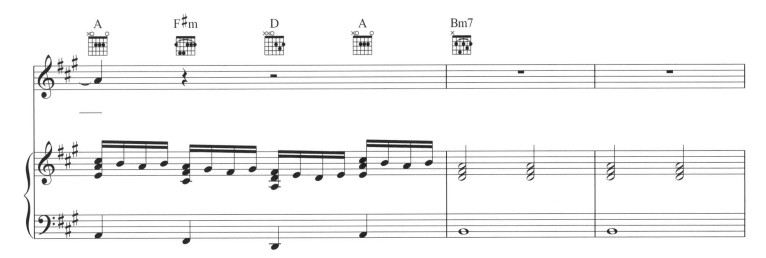

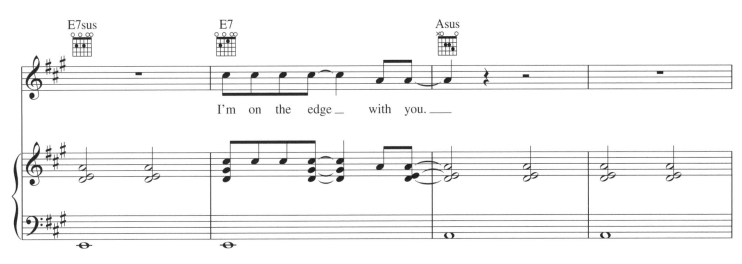

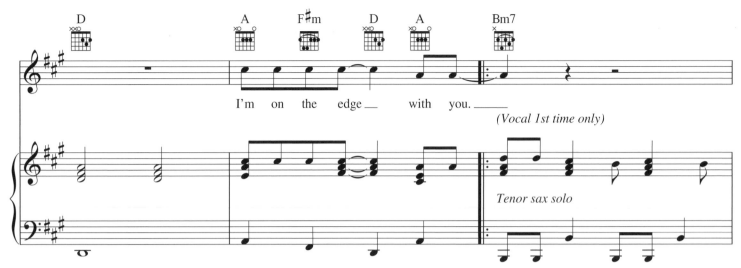

I'm on the edge ___ with you. ___

(Vocal 1st time only)

Tenor sax solo

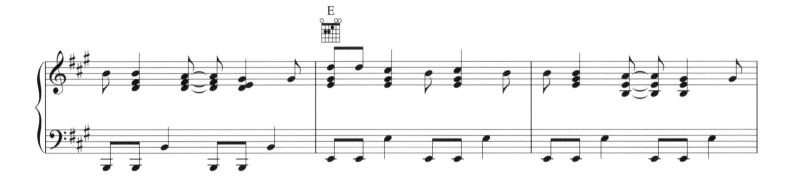

Sax solo ends

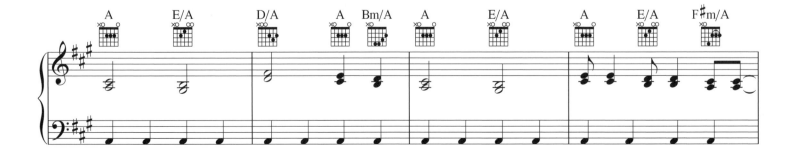

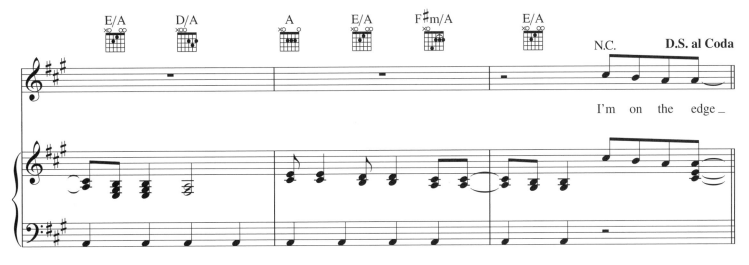

TONIGHT
(I'm Lovin' You)

Words and Music by CHRISTOPHER BRIDGES,
LAUREN CHRISTY, JUSTIN FRANKS
and JACOB LUTTRELL

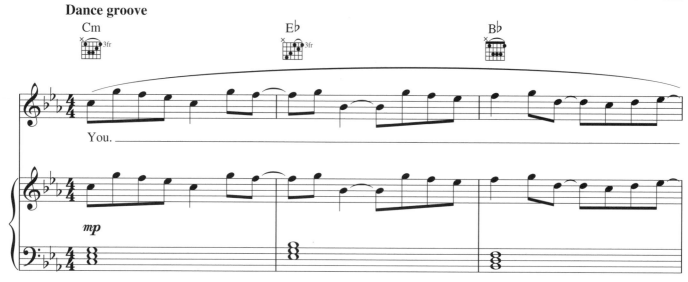

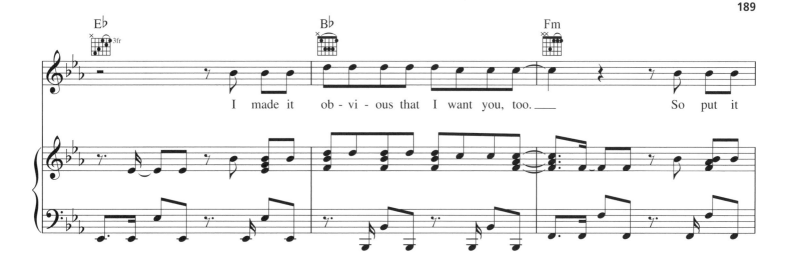

I made it ob-vi-ous that I want you, too.____ So put it

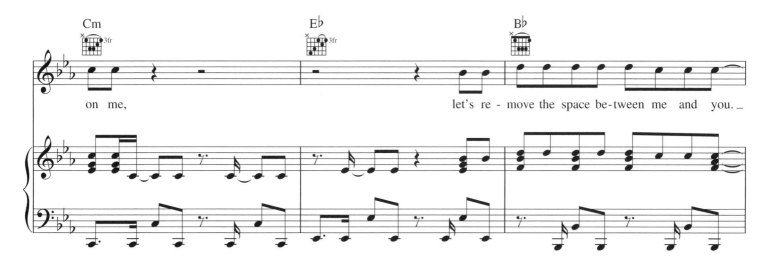

on me,____ let's re-move the space be-tween me and you.__

Now rock your bod-y, oh.____

Damn, I like the way that you move.__ So give it to me, oh,____

'cause I al-read-y know what you wan-na do.___ Here's the sit-u-

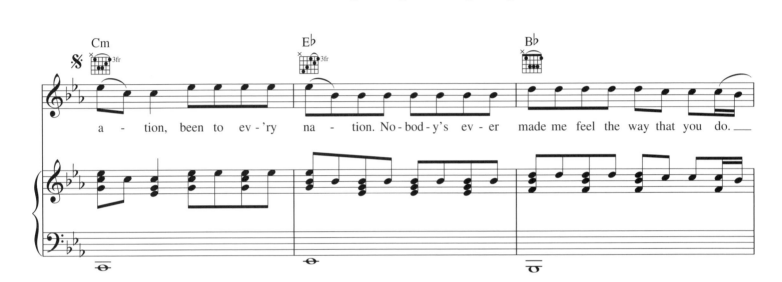

a-tion, been to ev-'ry na-tion. No-bod-y's ev-er made me feel the way that you do.___

You know my mo-ti-va-tion, giv-en my rep-u-ta-tion. Please ex-

cuse me, I don't mean to be rude,___ but to-night I'm lov-in' you.

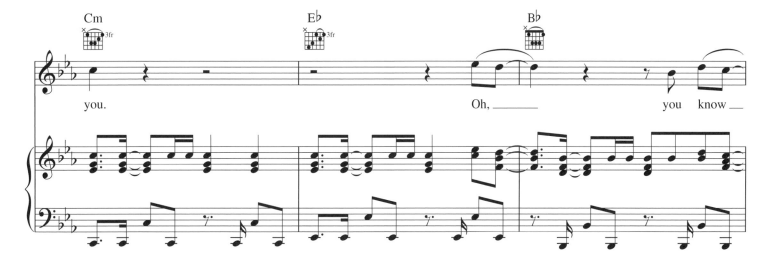

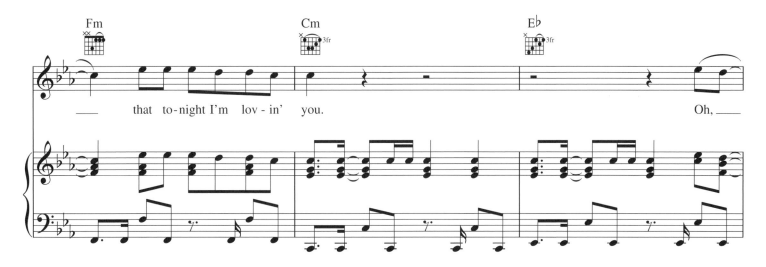

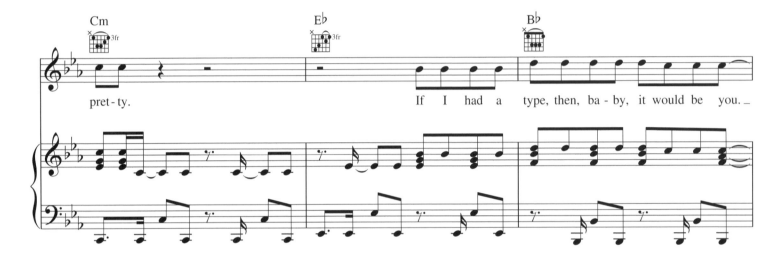

CODA

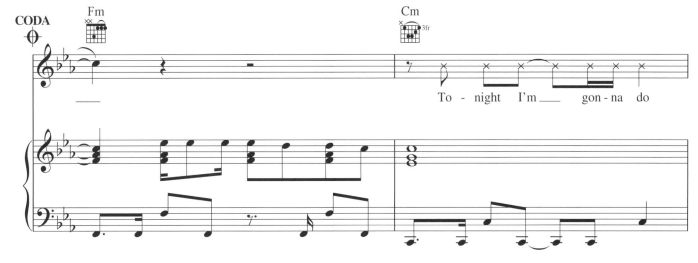

To - night I'm ___ gon - na do

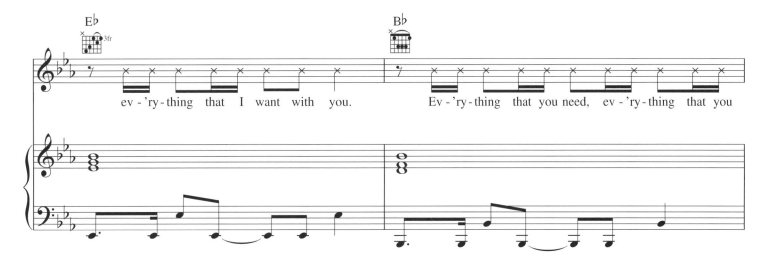

ev - 'ry - thing that I want with you.   Ev - 'ry - thing that you need, ev - 'ry - thing that you

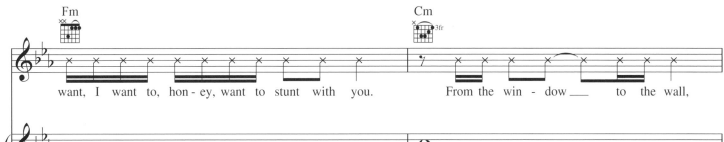

want, I want to, hon - ey, want to stunt with you.   From the win - dow ___ to the wall,

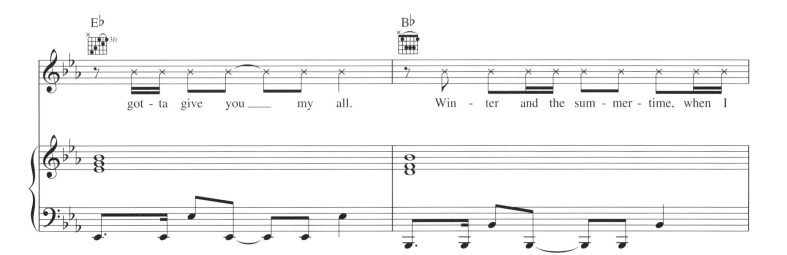

got - ta give you ___ my all.   Win - ter and the sum - mer - time, when I

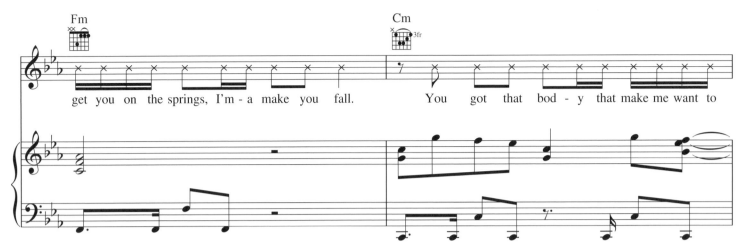

Fm · Cm

get you on the springs, I'm-a make you fall. You got that bod-y that make me want to

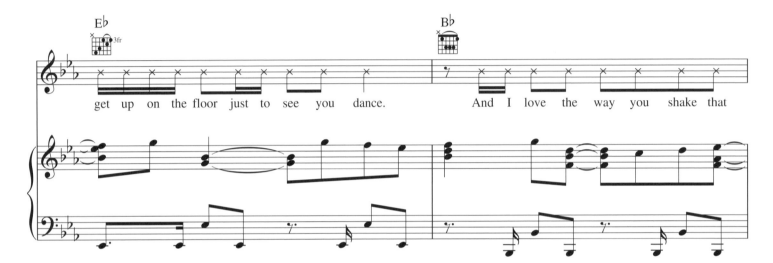

E♭ · B♭

get up on the floor just to see you dance. And I love the way you shake that

Fm · Cm

ass. Turn a-round and let me see them pants. You stuck with me, I'm stuck with

E♭ · B♭

you. Let's find some-thing to do. Please ex-cuse me, I don't mean to be rude, __

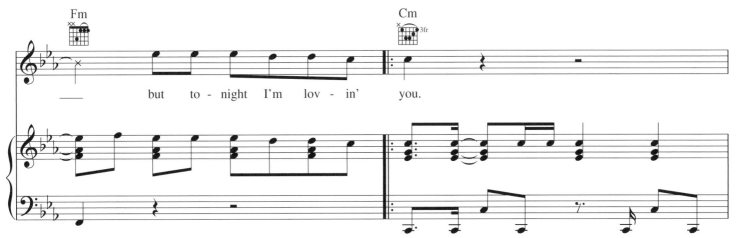

but to-night I'm lov-in' you.

Oh, _____ you know _____

that to-night I'm lov-in' you.

Oh, _____ you know _____ that to-night I'm lov-in'

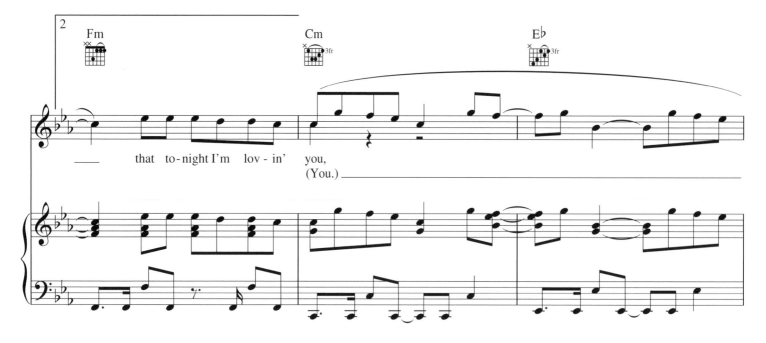

that to-night I'm lov-in' you,
(You.)

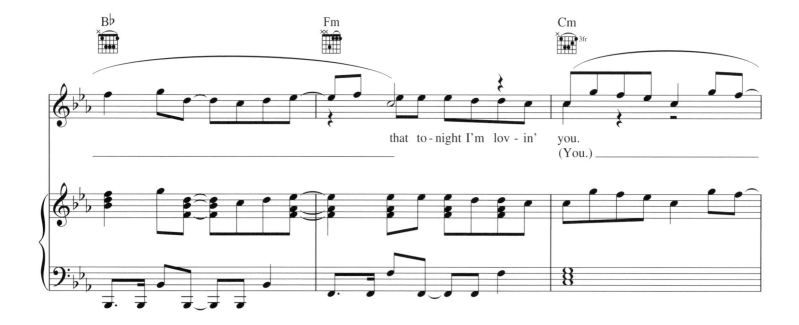

that to-night I'm lov-in' you.
(You.)

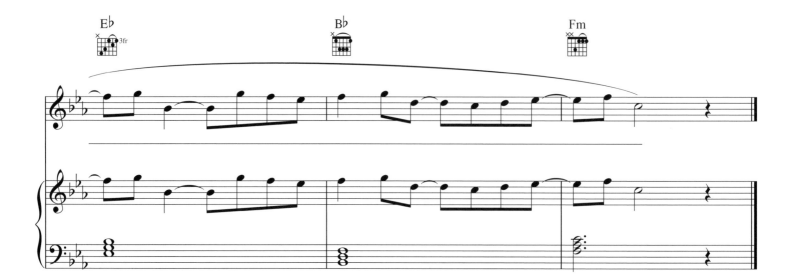

WE ARE FAMILY

Words and Music by NILE RODGERS
and BERNARD EDWARDS

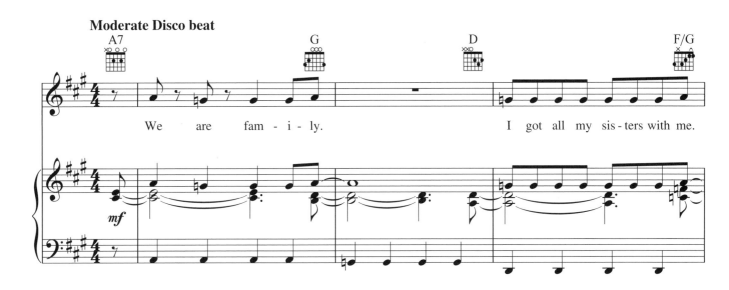

can see we're to - geth - er as we walk on by. ___

And we flock just like birds ___ of a feath -

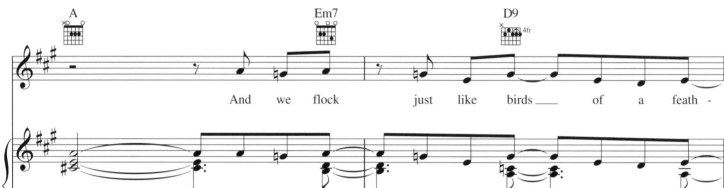

- er; I won't tell no lie. ___ All of the peo -

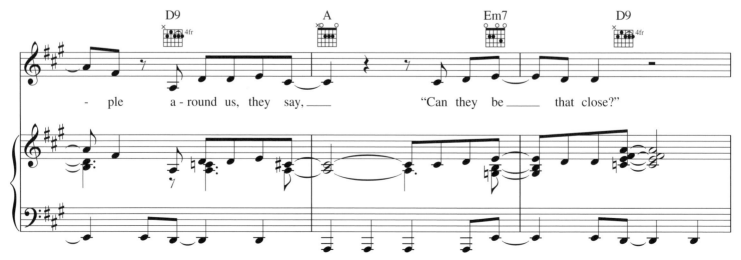

- ple a - round us, they say, ___ "Can they be ___ that close?"

TWIST AND SHOUT

Words and Music by BERT RUSSELL
and PHIL MEDLEY

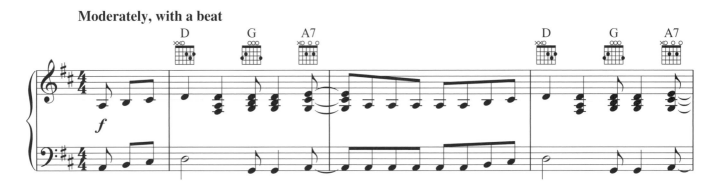

Well, shake it up, ba - by, __ now,
- by, __ now, (Shake it up, ba - by) Twist and
- by, __ now,

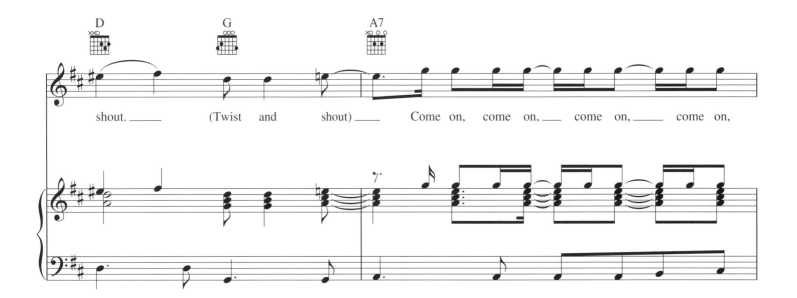

shout. __ (Twist and shout) __ Come on, come on, __ come on, __ come on,

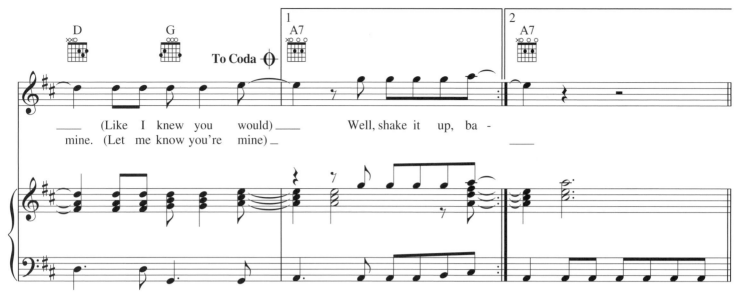

(Like I knew you would) ___ Well, shake it up, ba -
mine. (Let me know you're mine) ___

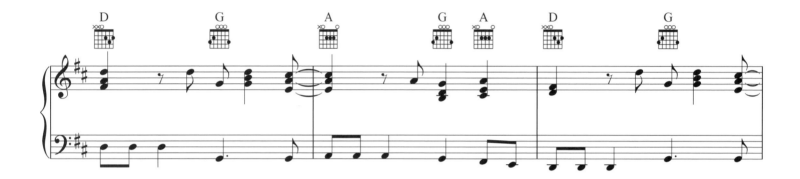

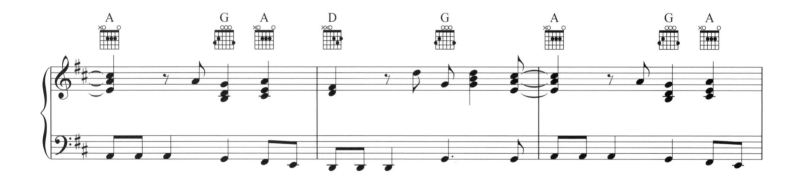

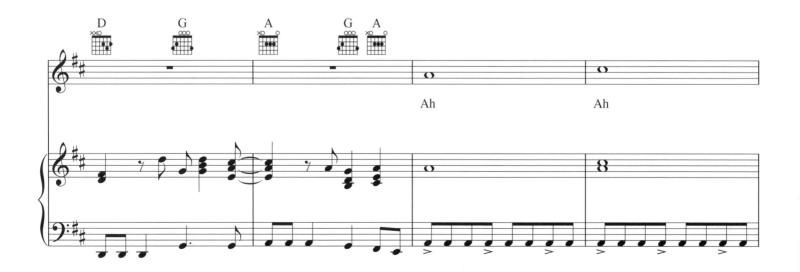

Ah   Ah

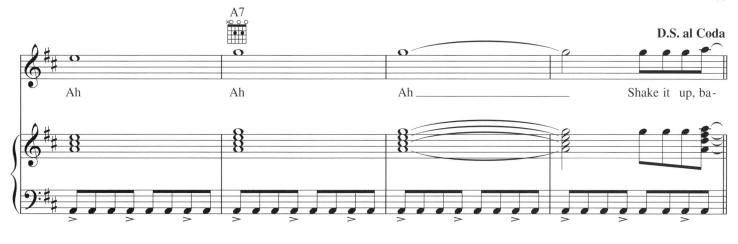

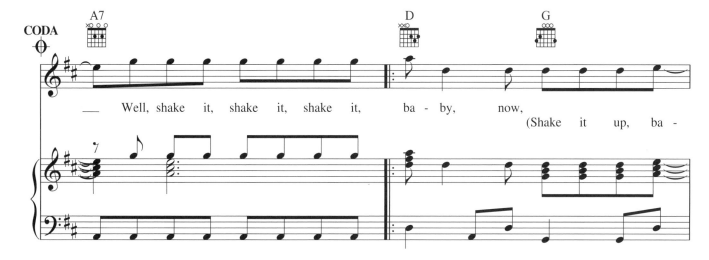

The Most Romantic Music In The World

Arranged for piano, voice, and guitar

The Best Love Songs Ever - 2nd Edition

This revised edition includes 65 romantic favorites: Always • Beautiful in My Eyes • Can You Feel the Love Tonight • Endless Love • Have I Told You Lately • Misty • Something • Through the Years • Truly • When I Fall in Love • and more.

00359198 .... $19.95

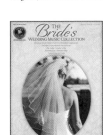

The Big Book of Love Songs - 2nd Edition

80 romantic hits in many musical styles: Always on My Mind • Cherish • Fields of Gold • I Honestly Love You • I'll Be There • Isn't It Romantic? • Lady • My Heart Will Go On • Save the Best for Last • Truly • Wonderful Tonight • and more.

00310784 .... $19.95

The Bride's Wedding Music Collection

A great collection of popular, classical and sacred songs for wedding musicians or engaged couples who are planning their service. Over 40 categorized songs, plus a website to hear audio clips! Songs include: Bless the Broken Road • Canon in D • Everything • Grow Old with Me • In My Life • Jesu, Joy of Man's Desiring • The Lord's Prayer • Marry Me • Ode to Joy • When You Say Nothing at All • and more.

00312298 .... $17.99

The Christian Wedding Songbook

37 songs of love and commitment, including: Bonded Together • Cherish the Treasure • Flesh of My Flesh • Go There with You • Household of Faith • How Beautiful • I Will Be Here • Love Will Be Our Home • Make Us One • Parent's Prayer • This Is the Day • This Very Day • and more.

00310681 .... $16.95

The Bride's Guide to Wedding Music - 2nd Edition

This great guide is a complete resource for planning wedding music. It includes a thorough article on choosing music for a wedding ceremony, and 65 songs in many different styles to satisfy lots of different tastes. The songs are grouped by categories, including preludes, processionals, recessionals, traditional sacred songs, popular songs, country songs, contemporary Christian songs, Broadway numbers, and new age piano music.

00310615 .... $19.95

Broadway Love Songs - 2nd Edition

This second edition features 47 sentimental favorites: Bells Are Ringing • Falling in Love with Love • From This Moment On • Goodnight, My Someone • Hello, Young Lovers • If I Loved You • Love Changes Everything • People Will Say We're in Love • Some Enchanted Evening • Where or When • more.

00311558 .... $15.95

Country Love Songs - 4th Edition

This edition features 34 romantic country favorites: Amazed • Breathe • Could I Have This Dance • Forever and Ever, Amen • I Need You • The Keeper of the Stars • Love Can Build a Bridge • One Boy, One Girl • Stand by Me • This Kiss • Through the Years • Valentine • You Needed Me • more.

00311528 .... $14.95

Love Songs

Budget Books Series

74 favorite love songs, including: And I Love Her • Cherish • Crazy • Endless Love • Fields of Gold • I Just Called to Say I Love You • I'll Be There • (You Make Me Feel Like) A Natural Woman • Wonderful Tonight • You Are So Beautiful • and more.

00310834 .... $12.99

The New Complete Wedding Songbook

41 of the most requested and beloved songs for romance and weddings: Anniversary Song • Ave Maria • Canon in D (Pachelbel) • Could I Have This Dance • Endless Love • I Love You Truly • Just the Way You Are • The Lord's Prayer • Through the Years • You Needed Me • Your Song • and more.

00309326 .... $12.95

New Ultimate Love and Wedding Songbook

This whopping songbook features 90 songs of devotion, including: The Anniversary Waltz • Can't Smile Without You • Could I Have This Dance • Endless Love • For All We Know • Forever and Ever, Amen • The Hawaiian Wedding Song • Here, There and Everywhere • I Only Have Eyes for You • Just the Way You Are • Longer • The Lord's Prayer • Love Me Tender • Misty • Somewhere • Sunrise, Sunset • Through the Years • Trumpet Voluntary • Your Song • and more.

00361445 .... $19.95

Romance - Boleros Favoritos

Features 48 Spanish and Latin American favorites: Aquellos Ojos Verdes • Bésame Mucho • El Reloj • Frenes • Inolvidable • La Vida Es Un Sueño • Perfidia • Siempre En Mi Corazón • Solamente Una Vez • more.

00310383 .... $16.95

Today's Hits for Weddings

Contains 25 of today's best pop and country hits that are perfect for weddings! Includes: Bless the Broken Road • Everything • Halo • I Do • Just the Way You Are • Love Story • Lucky • Marry Me • Mine • River of Love • Today Was a Fairytale • You Raise Me Up • and more.

00312316 .... $16.99

Valentine

Let your love light shine with this collection of 50 romantic favorites! Includes: Can't Help Falling and Love • Endless Love • If • Just the Way You Are • L-O-V-E • Mona Lisa • My Funny Valentine • Something • Three Coins in the Fountain • We've Only Just Begun • You Are So Beautiful • You'll Accomp'ny Me • and more!

00310977 .... $16.95

Selections from

VH1's 100 Greatest Love Songs

Nearly 100 love songs chosen for their emotion. Includes: Always on My Mind • Baby, I Love Your Way • Careless Whisper • Endless Love • How Deep Is Your Love • I Got You Babe • If You Leave Me Now • Love Me Tender • My Heart Will Go On • Unchained Melody • You're Still the One • and dozens more!

00306506 .... $27.95

HAL•LEONARD® CORPORATION

7777 W. BLUEMOUND RD. P.O. BOX 13819
MILWAUKEE, WISCONSIN 53213

www.halleonard.com

Prices, contents, and availability subject to change without notice.
Some products may not be available outside the U.S.A.

0312

Big Books of Music

Our "Big Books" feature big selections of popular titles under one cover, perfect for performing musicians, music aficionados or the serious hobbyist. All books are arranged for piano, voice, and guitar, and feature stay-open binding, so the books lie flat without breaking the spine.

BIG BOOK OF BALLADS – 2ND ED.
62 songs.
00310485 ....$19.95

BIG BOOK OF BIG BAND HITS
84 songs.
00310701 ....$22.99

BIG BOOK OF BLUEGRASS SONGS
70 songs.
00311484 ....$19.95

BIG BOOK OF BLUES
80 songs.
00311843 ....$19.99

BIG BOOK OF BROADWAY
70 songs.
00311658 ....$19.95

BIG BOOK OF CHILDREN'S SONGS
55 songs.
00359261 ....$16.99

GREAT BIG BOOK OF CHILDREN'S SONGS
76 songs.
00310002 ....$14.95

FANTASTIC BIG BOOK OF CHILDREN'S SONGS
66 songs.
00311062 ....$17.95

MIGHTY BIG BOOK OF CHILDREN'S SONGS
65 songs.
00310467 ....$14.95

REALLY BIG BOOK OF CHILDREN'S SONGS
63 songs.
00310372 ....$17.99

BIG BOOK OF CHILDREN'S MOVIE SONGS
66 songs.
00310731 ....$19.99

BIG BOOK OF CHRISTMAS SONGS – 2ND ED.
126 songs.
00311520 ....$19.95

BIG BOOK OF CLASSIC ROCK
77 songs.
00310801 ....$22.95

BIG BOOK OF CLASSICAL MUSIC
100 songs.
00310508 ....$19.99

BIG BOOK OF CONTEMPORARY CHRISTIAN FAVORITES – 3RD ED.
50 songs.
00312067 ....$21.99

BIG BOOK OF COUNTRY MUSIC – 2ND ED.
63 songs.
00310188 ....$19.95

BIG BOOK OF COUNTRY ROCK
64 songs.
00311748 ....$19.99

BIG BOOK OF EARLY ROCK N' ROLL
99 songs.
00310398 ....$19.95

BIG BOOK OF '50S & '60S SWINGING SONGS
67 songs.
00310982 ....$19.95

BIG BOOK OF FOLK POP ROCK
79 songs.
00311125 ....$24.95

BIG BOOK OF FRENCH SONGS
70 songs.
00311154 ....$19.95

BIG BOOK OF GERMAN SONGS
78 songs.
00311816 ....$19.99

BIG BOOK OF GOSPEL SONGS
100 songs.
00310604 ....$19.95

BIG BOOK OF HYMNS
125 hymns.
00310510 ....$17.95

BIG BOOK OF IRISH SONGS
76 songs.
00310981 ....$19.95

BIG BOOK OF ITALIAN FAVORITES
80 songs.
00311185 ....$19.99

BIG BOOK OF JAZZ – 2ND ED.
75 songs.
00311557 ....$19.95

BIG BOOK OF LATIN AMERICAN SONGS
89 songs.
00311562 ....$19.95

BIG BOOK OF LOVE SONGS
80 songs.
00310784 ....$19.95

BIG BOOK OF MOTOWN
84 songs.
00311061 ....$19.95

BIG BOOK OF MOVIE MUSIC
72 songs.
00311582 ....$19.95

BIG BOOK OF NOSTALGIA
158 songs.
00310004 ....$24.99

BIG BOOK OF OLDIES
73 songs.
00310756 ....$19.95

BIG BOOK OF RAGTIME PIANO
63 songs.
00311749 ....$19.95

BIG BOOK OF RHYTHM & BLUES
67 songs.
00310169 ....$19.95

BIG BOOK OF ROCK
78 songs.
00311566 ....$22.95

BIG BOOK OF ROCK BALLADS
67 songs.
00311839 ....$22.99

BIG BOOK OF SOUL
71 songs.
00310771 ....$19.95

BIG BOOK OF STANDARDS
86 songs.
00311667 ....$19.95

BIG BOOK OF SWING
84 songs.
00310359 ....$19.95

BIG BOOK OF TORCH SONGS – 2ND ED.
75 songs.
00310561 ....$19.99

BIG BOOK OF TV THEME SONGS
78 songs.
00310504 ....$19.95

BIG BOOK OF WEDDING MUSIC
77 songs.
00311567 ....$19.95

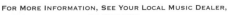